THE JOY OF THE JOURNEY

THE JOY OF THE JOURNEY

Ardeth Greene Kapp

Deseret Book Company
Salt Lake City, Utah

Library of Congress Cataloging-in-Publication Data

Kapp, Ardeth Greene, 1931–
    The joy of the journey / Ardeth Greene Kapp.
        p.   cm.
    Includes index.
    ISBN 0-87579-633-8
    1. Christian life—Mormon authors.   2. Kapp, Ardeth Greene,
1931–   . I. Title.
BX8656.K38   1992
248.4'89332—dc20   92-15839
                                                                         CIP

Printed in the United States of America
10   9   8   7   6   5   4   3   2   1

*To Heber, my husband, who adds joy
to the journey each day of my life*

Contents

Contents

Preface

We live in a time when we can do more, have more, see more, accumulate more, and want more than at any time we have ever known. I believe that if possible, the adversary would keep us busily engaged in a multitude of trivial things in an effort to keep us distracted from the few vital things that make all the difference.

Many of us live in expectation of better days ahead, next week, next month, or next year. We will feel joy when we reach this goal, accomplish that project, or acquire some possession. The anticipation of joy is often hoped for just around the next corner, when health improves, financial resources increase, or some promotion or position becomes ours. While it is important to plan for and look ahead to the future, it is quite possible that we shall miss the joy of the journey unless we are awakened to experience the good things in life that are often crowded out by the seeming demands and distractions of life. We may feel the need to schedule, program, and calendar good times when what we really need is to be awakened to the unprogrammed, unexpected, and beautiful things that take place each day.

The joy of the journey comes not only in the anticipation of our ultimate destination, but also when our eyes are opened and we learn to experience the wonders of life and the goodness of life even while we are faced with the challenges.

The journey through this mortal life is laced with joy and also afflictions. The scriptures teach us, "Men are, that they might have joy." (2 Nephi 2:25.) The Lord told Nephi, "Behold, I have refined thee, I have chosen thee in the furnace of affliction." (1 Nephi 20:10.) The Lord will come to us in our afflictions. He has covenanted with us to never desert us or leave us, and there is great joy in the knowledge that we can trust him. For us, it is just as he told the people in Alma's time: "I will also ease the burdens which are put upon your shoulders, that even you cannot feel them upon your backs, . . . and this I will do that ye may stand as witnesses for me hereafter, and that ye may know of a surety that I, the Lord God, do visit my people in their afflictions." (Mosiah 24:14.)

In these writings I share experiences found in the joy of the journey, with a desire that the readers might increase in their ability to find joy in their personal and daily lives.

There is joy in friendship, and the promises of friendship and friends now and forever. (See D&C 130:2.) There is joy in not having things always our way, but our Father's way, because of our trust in God and faith in his eternal plan. There is joy in repentance and forgiveness, and in knowing that our sins can be washed away and remembered no more. There is joy in the whisperings of the Spirit at times when the voices of the world would otherwise destroy our peace.

These stories tell of the joy experienced through a woman's righteous influence, the joy that comes from the light within, the joy in traveling together, the joy in keeping in touch with our heavenly home and in following the path provided by our Savior.

We are away from home, and on occasion we have feelings of homesickness. The way may seem long, but however steep the path, Jesus Christ, our Lord and Savior, will be with us. He set the pattern and invites us to follow him.

As we seek to do the will of our Father in heaven and strive to walk in his steps each day, we will come to understand the purpose of life and experience the joy of the journey.

Acknowledgments

I express appreciation to my husband, Heber, who encourages me to write and helps make time for my writing projects. I am grateful to Kerry Lin Hammond and Gerrie Mills, dear friends with secretarial skills, who have assisted me in the completion of this project. I express deepest gratitude and appreciation to Eleanor Knowles, executive editor of Deseret Book, who first encouraged me to publish and who continues to provide the skillful editing for my manuscripts.

A WOMAN'S
RIGHTEOUS INFLUENCE

CHAPTER 1

What Will You Make Room For in Your Wagon?

S ome time ago my niece Shelly called my home to report what sounded to me like a condition of epidemic proportion. It was just before finals, and Shelly explained that she and her roommates were stressed out and needed a place to escape for the weekend. I, of course, was happy to provide such a place. They told me there had hardly been a weekend or even a day when they had not been completely overloaded. "So much to do and so little time" was their comment, as they talked of schedules, commitments, expectations, pressures, and even some anxieties about dates, deadlines, decisions, finances, future obligations, and unlimited opportunities.

With so many wonderful opportunities, maybe one could take advantage of it all if you could stay up long enough, get up early enough, run fast enough, and live long enough. It has been said that if you're willing to burn the candle at both ends, you might get by, but only if the candle is long enough.

We all seem to be looking for ways to do more faster. Nowadays we can watch one TV show while we tape another and fast forward to eliminate the commercials. We read condensed books and eat fast foods. Some would have us believe that the more appointments we have in our day planner, the more successful we are. The plague of our day is the thought that crowds into our mind like the steady ticking of a clock repeated over and over: "I do not have time. I do not have time." And yet we have all the time there is.

3

Today we read of stress management, the Epstein-Barr Syndrome, overload, and over-exhaustion. As people try to escape some of the pressures, there is an increased consumption of alcohol, the improper use of prescription drugs and other related social ills, immorality, and even suicide.

And yet never before has there been such evidence of increased knowledge and expanding opportunities. In his book *Megatrends,* author John Naisbitt says, "We have exploded into a free-wheeling multiple-option society." (New York: Warner Books, 1982, p. xxiii.) We are faced with the burden of too many choices. I have discovered that even the purchase of a simple tube of toothpaste poses many options, considering brand, flavor, size, cost, ingredients, and promises. We speak of high tech and high touch, hardware and software, and find the need for increasing self-reliance as the options multiply at an accelerated pace.

William James, the noted American psychologist, stated, "Neither the nature nor the amount of our work is accountable for the frequency and severity of our breakdowns. But their cause lies rather in those absurd feelings of hurry and having no time, breathless, tension, anxiety, the lack of inner harmony and peace."

Too often we allow ourselves to be driven from one deadline, activity, or opportunity to the next. We check events off our calendar and say to ourselves, "After this week things will let up," or "After such and such happens, the pressure will ease." We live with false expectations. Unless we learn to take control of the present, we will always live in anticipation of better days in the future. And when those days arrive, we shall still be looking ahead, making it difficult to enjoy the here and now. The beautiful fall leaves come and go, and in our busyness we miss them. "Given another season, we'll do better," we say.

We live in a time when we can do more, have more, see more, accumulate more, and want more than any other time we have ever known. I believe that if possible, the adversary would keep us busily engaged in a multitude of trivial things in an effort to keep us distracted from the few vital things that make *all* of the difference. When we take control of our lives, we refuse to give up what we want most even if it means giving up some of what we want now. In a talk at Brigham Young University, former BYU president Jeffrey R. Holland reminded students that Christ expects us to "postpone gratification, indefinitely if necessary, rather than appease [our] appetite." ("The Inconvenient Messiah," *However Long and Hard the Road,* Salt Lake City: Deseret Book, 1985, p. 18.)

And how is this to be accomplished? I believe that the most destructive threat of our day is not nuclear war, not famine, not economic disaster; rather it is the despair, the discouragement, the despondency, the defeat caused by the discrepancy between what we believe to be right and how we live our lives. Much of the emotional and social illness of our day is caused when people think one way and act another. The turmoil inside is destructive to the Spirit and to the emotional well-being of one who tries to live without clearly defined principles, values, standards, and goals.

Principles are mingled with a sense of values. They magnify each other. Learning to like and dislike what we ought to like and striving to live the good life depend upon values to measure our progress. We learn to be honest by habit, as a matter of course. The question shouldn't be "What will people think?" but "What will I think of myself?" We must each have our own clearly defined values burning brightly within. Values provide an inner court to which we can appeal for judgment of our performance and our choices.

We live in a time when success is too often determined by the things we gather, accumulate, collect, measure, and even compare in relation to what others gather, accumulate, collect, measure, and compare. This pattern of living invites its own consequences and built-in stress. Perhaps you have heard of the woman who received a call from her banker explaining that she was overdrawn, to which she promptly replied, "No sir, I am not overdrawn. My husband may have underdeposited, but I am not overdrawn."

It is possible that we try to overdraw from our time bank and suffer the nagging and debilitating stress of bankruptcy. The difference, however, is more significant than our money bank. Only twenty-four hours a day is deposited for an indefinite period of time. No more and no less.

It is as we learn to simplify and reduce, set priorities, and cut back on excesses that we have enough time and money for the essentials, for all that we ultimately want in the end and even more.

Recently some friends came to our home with their children and brought a case of the most beautiful peaches I have ever seen. Brother Pitt explained that his family had just won first prize at the county fair for their peaches, and they had an orchard full of them. I asked how one produced such remarkable fruit, and they were eager to explain. "We learned how to prune the peach trees and thin the weak fruit," they said. "It's hard work and must be done regularly." "We also learned what happens when you don't prune," said one of the children. Their father had wisely suggested that three trees in the orchard be left to grow without the harsh results of the pruning knife. The children explained to me that the fruit from these trees was not only very small but also did not have the sweet taste of the other fruit. The lesson was obvious. There was no question in their minds about the far-reaching value of careful pruning.

In an ethics conference sponsored by the Marriott School of Management at BYU, McKinley Tabor reflected regretfully on some misplaced priorities. He said, "I was aggressive in wanting to own things, in wanting to make a lot of money, in wanting to be the big duck in a little pond. Now I focus on things like my children, on my family life in general, on experiencing things instead of owning things. I like to go places and see new things and meet new people where before I liked to own cars and have big bank accounts. The things that are important to me now are things that stay with you a lot longer than a dollar bill." ("Misplaced Pride," *BYU Today*, July 1989, pp. 17–19.)

In his book *The Star Thrower*, Loren Eiseley writes about the beaches of Costabel and tells of how tourists and professional shell collectors, with a kind of greedy madness, begin to gather, collect, and compete early in the morning, in an attempt to outrun their less-aggressive neighbors. After a storm, people are seen hurrying along with bundles, gathering starfish in their sacks. Following one such episode, the writer says:

> I met the star thrower. . . . He was gazing fixedly at something in the sand. Eventually he stooped and flung the object beyond the breaking surf.
> "Do you collect?" [I asked].
> "Only like this," he said softly. . . . "And only for the living."
> He stooped again, oblivious of my curiosity, and skipped another star neatly across the water. "The stars," he said, "throw well. One can help them."
> For a moment, in the changing light, the sower appeared magnified, as though casting larger stars upon some greater sea. He had, at any rate, the posture of a god. . . .
> I picked and flung a star. I could have thrown in a frenzy of joy, but I set my shoulders and cast, as the thrower in the rainbow cast, slowly, deliberately, and well. The task was not to be assumed lightly, for it was men as well as starfish that we sought to save. (New York: Harcourt Brace Jovanovich, 1978, pp. 171–72, 184.)

While gatherers carry bags weighed down with the accumulation of their possessions, star throwers find their joy in picking up those that would otherwise die on the sandy beach.

Like the Star Thrower, those who have nothing visible to show for their labors are often individuals who are filled, rewarded, and energized by a labor that invigorates, motivates, inspires, and has a purpose of such far-reaching significance that they are driven by a power beyond themselves. This power is most often felt when we are in the service of our fellow beings, for in that service, as King Benjamin taught, we are in the service of our God. (Mosiah 2:17.)

We read about the pioneers who, in the early history of the Church, left their possessions and headed west. Those who were with the handcart company had to give much thought to what they would make room for in their carts and what they would be willing to leave behind. Even after the journey began, some things had to be unloaded along the way if people were to reach their destination.

In our season of abundance and excess, while we are counseled to reduce and simplify, there will be a high level of frustration until we understand the value of pruning. When someone asks, "How do you do it all?" our answer should be, "I don't." We must be willing to let go of many things but defend with our lives the essentials.

I believe it would be very easy for an inexperienced gardener to approach the task of reducing and cutting back with such vigor that he might take a saw and cut a tree down the center, through the trunk, and into the roots. Surely it would be cut back, but what of the hope for the fruit? Wise pruning, like good gardening, takes careful thought. It is only when we are clear in our minds concerning our values that we are free to simplify and reduce without putting at risk what matters most. Until we determine what is of greatest worth, we are caught up in the unrealistic idea that everything is possible.

Thomas Griffith, a contributing editor for *Time,* once summarized the problem this way: "I thought myself happy [as a young man], my head full of every popular song that came along, the future before me. I could be an artist, a great novelist, an architect, a senator, a singer; having no demonstrable capacity for any of these pursuits made them all appear equally possible to me. All that mattered, I felt, was my inclination; I saw life as a set of free choices. Only later did it occur to me that every road taken is another untaken, every choice a narrowing. A sadder maturity convinces me that, as in a chess game, every move helps commit one to the next, and each person's situation at a given moment is the sum of the moves he has made before." (*The Waist-High Culture,* New York: Harper and Brothers, 1959, p. 17.)

When we decide what is essential, we are released from the gripping position of doubtful indecision and confusion. It is while a person stands undecided, uncommitted, uncovenanted, with choices waiting to be made, that the vulnerability of every wind that blows becomes life threatening. Uncertainty, the thief of time and commitment, breeds vacillation and confusion.

When our choices and decisions are focused on the accumulation of visible possessions and valuable materials, we may find that the acquisition of these things feeds an insatiable appetite and leaves us increasingly hungry. In the Book of Mormon the Lord warns us: "Wherefore, do not spend money for that which is of no worth, nor your labor for that which cannot satisfy. Hearken diligently unto me, and remember the words which I have spoken; and come unto the Holy One of Israel, and feast upon that which perisheth not, neither can be corrupted, and let your soul delight in fatness." (2 Nephi 9:51.)

When our time is spent in the accumulation of experiences that nourish the spirit, we see with different glasses things that others do not see and cannot understand.

In the book *The Little Prince,* we read about the importance of values and relationships. The fox says to the Little Prince, "It is only with the heart that one can see rightly; what is essential is invisible to the eye." (Antoine De Saint-Exupéry, *The Little Prince,* New York: Harcourt, Brace & World, 1943, p. 70.)

One of the great examples of acquiring invisible possessions of priceless value comes from the dramatic story told of the early pioneers known as Zion's Camp. The Saints in Missouri were expelled from Jackson County in late November 1833. Four months and twelve days later, February 24, 1834, Joseph Smith was instructed to organize an army in Kirtland, Ohio, to go to Missouri and help the Missouri Saints regain their property in Jackson County. The group he led, Zion's Camp, marched one thousand miles in four months and suffered sickness, deprivation, and severe testing of every physical kind.

"Elder Heber C. Kimball of the Quorum of the Twelve said, 'I took leave of my wife and children and friends, not knowing whether I would see them again in the flesh.' . . . It was not unusual for [the small army] to march thirty-five miles a day, despite blistered feet, oppressive heat, heavy rains, high humidity, hunger, and thirst. Armed guards were posted around the camp at night. At 4:00 A.M. the trumpeter roused the weary men with reveille on an old, battered French horn. . . . Zion's Camp failed to help the Missouri Saints regain their lands and was marred by some dissension, apostasy, and unfavorable publicity, but a number of positive results came from the journey. . . . Zion's Camp chastened, polished, and spiritually refined many of the Lord's servants. . . . When a skeptic asked what he had gained from his journey, Brigham Young promptly replied, 'I would not exchange the knowledge I have received this season for the whole of Geauga County.' " (*Church History in the Fulness of Times,* Salt Lake City: Church Educational System, 1989, pp. 143, 151.)

From among the members of Zion's Camp, the Lord selected those who would lead his church during the next five decades. From the viewpoint of preparation, the Zion's Camp experiences proved to be of infinite value during the formative years of the Church. Those Saints were tried and tested. They learned what they stood for, what they were willing to live and die for, and what was of highest value.

Today our tests are different. We are not called to load our wagons and head west. Our frontier and wilderness are of a different nature, but we too must decide what we will make room for in our wagons and what is of highest value.

The Museum of Church History and Art in Salt Lake City features an exhibit entitled "A Covenant Restored." As we enter, we begin to remember in a new way the price paid by those who came before us. Standing at the edge of a very rough-hewn log cabin, we feel something of the commitment and sacrifice

10

those early Saints made. Next to this very humble dwelling, where life was sustained by men and women with values, commitments, and covenants, is a replica in actual size of a beautiful window in the historic Kirtland Temple.

Moving along the path through the museum, we are drawn emotionally from Kirtland on through the experiences that finally brought the Saints to the valley of the Great Salt Lake. At one point we see the temple as the center of everything that drove them through these incredible circumstances, and we begin to feel, in ways that perhaps we haven't before, the significance of the temple in their lives and ours.

As I visited the exhibit and stood at the side of a handcart, I wondered: How did the family decide what they would make room for in their wagons? And what will we make room for in our wagons? What is of greatest importance in life?

One year as I was driving back to Utah from a trip to Vernon, British Columbia, I had an experience that has helped me as I try to improve my ability to prune wisely and to load or unload my wagon, as the case may be. With me was my niece Shelly, who was then seven years old, and when we were not playing a tape of "Winnie the Pooh," she would be asleep in the back seat of the car. Thus I had many hours and many miles to weigh, compare, and wonder. I had gone to Canada to take care of my sister's family of nine children while she was in the hospital with her tenth baby. After a week of doing laundry, matching socks, tending to paper routes, meals, lessons, car pooling, bedtime stories, and lunch money, settling disputes over time spent in the bathroom, finding shoes, and planning for family home evening, I felt overwhelmed, to say the least. At the appointed time my sister returned with a babe in arms. I stood in awe and reverence as I watched her step back into that routine with the ease and harmony of a conductor leading a well-trained orchestra. It was a miracle to me.

As I thought of her life and mine, I began comparing what I was not doing with what she *was* doing, and I began to feel discouraged, despondent, and even depressed.

At that moment, somewhere between the Canadian border and Spokane, my father's voice came into my mind. He had passed away two years before, but his voice was as clear as though he were sitting by my side. "My dear," he said, "don't worry about the little things — and the big things you agreed to before you came." And for the rest of the journey, between moments of listening to Winnie the Pooh, I asked myself over and over again, What are the big things in life? What is essential? What is the purpose of life?

The years have passed since that experience, and Shelly has traded Winnie the Pooh for the more important things. She has served a mission to New Zealand, leaving important things behind, including ballroom dancing, which for Shelly borders on being essential, to go forth and teach the real essentials, the gospel of Jesus Christ.

Elder John A. Widtsoe wrote: "In our pre-existent state, in the day of the great council, we made a certain agreement with the Almighty. The Lord proposed a plan, conceived by him. We accepted it. Since the plan is intended for all men, we become parties to the salvation of every person under that plan. We agreed, right then and there, to be not only saviors for ourselves, but measurably saviors for the whole human family. We went into a partnership with the Lord." (*Utah Genealogical and Historical Magazine*, October 1943, p. 289.)

The working out of the plan became then not merely the Father's work, and the Savior's work, but also our work. The least of us, the humblest, is in partnership with the Almighty in achieving the purpose of the eternal plan of salvation. That places us in a very responsible attitude toward the human race.

Like the Star Thrower, it is in helping to save others that we find our pleasure and joy, our labor and ultimately our glory. Elder Widtsoe further stated: "If the Lord's concern is chiefly to bring happiness and joy, salvation, to the whole human family, we cannot become like the Father unless we too engage in that work. There is no chance for the narrow, selfish, introspective man in the kingdom of God. He may survive in the world of men; he may win fame, fortune and power before men, but he will not stand high before the Lord unless he learns to do the works of God, which always points toward the salvation of the whole human family." (Ibid.)

Our understanding of and commitment to the covenants we have made with God are the essentials. Our day-to-day interactions, our integrity, our moral conduct, our willingness to "bear one another's burdens, that they may be light, . . . and . . . to mourn with those that mourn, . . . and comfort those that stand in need of comfort, and to stand as witnesses of God at all times and in all things, and in all places" (Mosiah 18:8–9) are at the very heart of our earth-life experience. Every decision should be made with that goal in mind, and we should expect it to be difficult. We are to be tried and tested in all things. (See D&C 136:31.)

Some time ago, my husband and I visited the Mormon cemetery at Winter Quarters, Nebraska, a monument to Latter-day Saint pioneers young and old who were buried in graves along the trail as their families continued westward toward the Rocky Mountains. Of those people who had vision and faith in God, we read: "There are times and places in the life of every individual, every people, and every nation when great spiritual heights are reached, when courage becomes a living thing . . . when faith in God stands as the granite mountain wall, firm and immovable. . . . Winter Quarters was such a time and place for the Mormon people." (Heber J. Grant, remarks at the dedication of the Winter Quarters Monument, 1936.)

A person who only looks for the visible may draw from this pioneer experience what appears to be an obvious conclusion: families perished. But in the eternal perspective, they did not. It was their willingness to sacrifice everything, even life if necessary, that would ensure the eternal lives of these families.

And what of our Winter Quarters and Zion's Camp experiences? Times of difficulty try the faith of all who profess to be Latter-day Saints and follow the prophets. We are walking in the well-worn paths of those who preceded us in the quest for

13

Zion. Help and comfort are available to us through sources beyond our own immediate strength, just as they were for those who have gone before us.

To become saints, we must endure trials. Through our covenant relationship with Jesus Christ we do all that we can do, and by the grace of God he does the rest.

One of the early pioneers testified, "I have pulled my handcart when I was so weak and weary from illness and lack of food that I could hardly put one foot ahead of the other. I have looked ahead and seen a patch of sand or a hill slope, and I have said, 'I can go only that far and there I must give up for I cannot pull the load through it.' . . . I have gone on to that sand and when I reached it, the cart began pushing me. I have looked back many times to see who was pushing my cart, but my eyes saw no one. I knew then that the angels of God were there." (*Relief Society Magazine*, January 1948, p. 8.)

It is with faith in God that we must condition ourselves to let go of everything, if necessary. For some of us this may require unloading bad habits, attitudes, disobedience, arrogance, selfishness, and pride.

Recently our family came into possession of the first letter written to my grandmother by her mother when my grandmother left her home in England as a young immigrant. She left everything behind because someone taught her the gospel of Jesus Christ. For fear of being persuaded to remain in England, she did not tell her family of her conversion to the Church or her plans to leave until after she left for America. She joined the Saints in America and eventually moved to Canada. That first letter received from her mother reads in part:

"My dearest daughter . . . whatever on earth has caused you to go out of your own country and away from all your friends, I cannot imagine. You say, 'Don't fret.' How do you think I can help it when such a blow as that come to struck me all up in a heap? You say you are happy, but I can't think it, for I am sure I could not have been happy to have gone into a foreign country and left you behind. You say you will come again, but

I don't think you will hesitate your life over the deep waters again. When I think about it, I feel wretched. You had a good place and a good home to come to whenever you liked. And I must say that I loved the very ground you walked upon, and now I am left to fret in this world. But still, all the same for that, I wish you good luck and hope the Lord will prosper you in every way. I remain, your loving Mother."

My grandmother never saw her mother again in this earth life, and none of her family joined the Church. However, their temple work has been done for them.

What is it that drives a people to sacrifice all if necessary to receive the blessings available only in the temple? It is their faith and their spiritual witness of the importance of covenants with God and the immense possibilities they open up to us. In the temple, the house of the Lord, we may participate in ordinances and covenants that span the distance between heaven and earth and prepare us to return to God's presence and enjoy the blessings of eternal families and eternal life.

A few weeks after my visit to the Kirtland Temple, I stood at the water's edge of the baptismal font in the small Manila Temple in the Philippines. Many of those dear Saints had traveled by boat for three days, in intense heat and humidity, to come and participate in sacred ordinances available only in the temple. In a small, primitive nipa hut on one of these islands, I visited with a family of Latter-day Saints. A beautiful young fourteen-year-old in this humble setting listened intently while her father explained that by saving all they could, within a year or so the family would have enough to go to the temple to be sealed as a family forever.

When we understand that our covenants with God are essential to our eternal life, these sacred promises become the driving force that helps us lighten our load, set priorities on our activities, eliminate the excesses, accelerate our progress, and reduce the distractions that could, if not guarded, get us mired down in mud while other wagons move on. If we become burdened with sin and sorrow, transgression and guilt, we need to unload our wagon and fill it with obedience, faith, hope, and a regular renewal of our covenants with God. President Kimball reminded us, "Since immortality and eternal life constitute the sole purpose of life, all other interests and activities are but incidental thereto." (*The Miracle of Forgiveness*, Salt Lake City: Bookcraft, 1969, p. 2.)

Does that suggest there should be no football, fashion, fancy food, or fun? Of course not. But these things are incidental to the real purpose of our earth life, which provides the compass and keeps us on course while we enjoy the journey. If we are found to be long-faced, sober, and sanctimonious, we will be guilty of portraying a false image of the joys of the gospel. As the pioneers traveled, they enjoyed singing and dancing. In their camaraderie, they built a community with a strong sense of brotherhood and sisterhood. People with common values and goals strengthened one another in joy and sorrow, in sickness and health. They sustained one another as they prepared to make and keep sacred covenants. A unique strength comes when a group of faithful saints, however large or small, band together and encourage each other in righteousness.

As we take an inventory of the things we are carrying in our wagons and make decisions about what we will be willing to leave behind and what we will cling to, we have guidance. The Lord has given us a great promise. He has said, "Therefore, if you will ask of me you shall receive; if you will knock it shall be opened unto you. Seek to bring forth and establish my Zion. Keep my commandments in all things. And, if you keep my commandments and endure to the end you shall have eternal life, which gift is the greatest of all the gifts of God." (D&C 14:5–7.)

We live in a time when the things of the world would, if possible, press in upon us and close out the things of God. May we turn our attention from the glitter of the world as we give thanks for the glory of the gospel.

CHAPTER 2

Love Makes the
World Go Around

S ome time ago I received a letter from a young woman who wrote, "Dear Sister Kapp: I have a problem. Could you please advise me on how to encourage the boys I like and discourage the boys I don't like? I'm anxious to know."

In my response I warned her to be very careful, because the boy she doesn't like this week might be the one she will like next. That's called falling in and out of love, romantic love. I suggested she try to like all of the boys and all of the girls all of the time, in every season. As I consider that counsel, I'd like to recommend it for each of us.

We've all seen the familiar symbol that communicates the idea of love without any words. We see it on bumper stickers and T-shirts. It is simply the word "I" followed by the shape of a heart and then the word of something someone loves. For example, we read "I love [represented by a heart] snow," or chocolate, or whatever. Hearts signify love in nearly every language.

Early one morning I awakened and walked out on my front porch to look at my flowers. To my surprise I discovered paper hearts stuck all over the front of our house—little hearts, big hearts, red hearts, pink hearts, placed high and low, all over, from one side of the porch to the other. I counted them. There were one hundred in all. On the front door was a very large heart with bold lettering that read, "You're having a heart attack." On the porch was a small basket filled with heart-shaped cookies and a little note with this message: "We love you, Sister Kapp."

I sat down on the porch, in my bathrobe, in my bare feet, and wondered, "Who did this? Why? What's the occasion? What have I done to deserve such attention?" It wasn't my birthday or Valentine's Day, just an ordinary day—that is, until I became invaded with hearts. I can assure you, I did not remove the hearts quickly. The cookies, yes, but not the hearts. They remained until the setting sun turned the red hearts to pink and the pink to almost white. Neighbors called across the street, "What's the special occasion?" I called back, "Someone loves me," and it felt good just to say that. I didn't discover until several days later that the Laurels from a ward in another stake had come clear across town very early that morning with their hands full of hearts, masking tape, cookies, and love. Love does make the world go around. It certainly made my world go around that day, and each time I think about it.

Eventually I decided to remove the hearts that had created so much attention and happy feelings in our neighborhood. By then they were faded and some slightly torn, but I could not bring myself to throw them away. They lay stacked on a shelf in the garage for several months. One day these faded hearts were called into service once again to perpetuate their message of love. At our family reunion that summer, Uncle Jack and Aunt Nina, the eldest members of the clan, parked their motor home not far from the cabin housing most of the people and all the commotion. In the silence of the night, family members of all ages, with one hundred faded hearts in hand, crept over to the camper and quietly covered the motor home. One large heart on the door said, "You're having a heart attack," and another one said, "We love you."

We all watched excitedly the following morning while Aunt Nina helped Uncle Jack, who had suffered a serious heart attack just months before, step down from the motor home. Then, getting their bearings, they turned around and saw their motor home covered with hearts. "We love you!" everyone shouted.

Those hearts had done it again. Tears filled the eyes of many, and we all experienced that tender, wonderful feeling of love.

On one occasion, after a rather large Young Women conference where I think I must have hugged over five hundred young women, I received a letter in the mail that read, "After you spoke to us, I waited in line, and when it was my turn, you hugged me and said something wonderful to me. I forgot what it was. Could you please write and tell me so I can put it in my journal and read it when I feel low?" I couldn't remember exactly what I whispered to her as I hugged her, but often I will say something like, "I love you very much, and I'll take you home with me in my heart." Was it the words she wanted to remember—or the feeling of being loved?

What is this thing called love, which is so essential to our well-being, our happiness, our growth, and our spirituality? The greatest of all the commandments our Father in heaven has given us deals with love. We read in the scriptures that a lawyer, one of the Pharisees, asked the Savior, "Master, which is the great commandment in the law? Jesus said unto him, Thou shalt love the Lord thy God with all thy heart, and with all thy soul, and with all thy mind. This is the first and great commandment. And the second is like unto it, Thou shalt love thy neighbour as thyself. On these two commandments hang all the law and the prophets." (Matthew 22:36–40.)

Love forms our foundation, our anchor, our mainstay, our security, and our defense. It should be the focal point for our life, at the top of every New Year's resolution and in the heart of every soul.

In a lecture at Brigham Young University, author Raymond Moody stated that he had interviewed one hundred people who had died and returned to life. They all responded that they followed a bright light and then were asked, "How have you loved and how have you served?" What would our answer be if we were asked to give an accounting of how we have loved and how we have served this past year? Will it read any differently for the coming year?

As Latter-day Saints, we are a covenant people. We have covenanted to take upon us the name of Christ and "to come into the fold of God, and to be called his people." (See Mosiah 18:8–10.)

In that upper room at the time of the Last Supper, the Savior of the world, knowing what was imminent — and at a time when he might have been concerned for his own welfare — spoke to the apostles gathered there (and through the scriptures, to each of us) of love. "A new commandment I give unto you," he said, "that ye love one another; as I have loved you, that ye also love one another." (John 13:34.) Can we in any possible way comprehend even in part the way the Savior loves us? He loves us unconditionally, the sinner and the saint. He gave his life for us. "He was wounded for our transgressions, he was bruised for our iniquities; the chastisement of our peace was upon him; and with his stripes we are healed." (Mosiah 14:5.) Through his atonement, a sinner can become a saint.

I struggle with how far I am from approaching that goal or even in some small way being able to comprehend the magnitude and magnificence of that divine, unconditional, unreserved, constant love of God. Even when I make resolves and fall short, I know he will never give up on me or you. Never, ever. The love that God has for us cries out for us to prove our love for him so he can bless us and help us and enlarge our spirit within. Love is of such importance that it becomes a distinguishing feature of those who profess to be disciples of Christ. He said, "By this shall all men know that ye are my disciples, if ye have love one to another." (John 13:35.) This is not just for us and our closest friends, but for all of our brothers and sisters, everywhere, always.

Most clubs, organizations, societies, fraternities, and sororities have some distinguishing features that set them apart from the rest. We take pride in our identity, especially if our group is exclusive. A favorite book of mine is *Adventures in Friendship* by David Grayson. I'd like to share with you a few excerpts from a chapter entitled "An Adventure in Fraternity":

This, I am firmly convinced, is a strange world, as strange a one as I was ever in. Looking about me I perceive that the simplest things are the most difficult, the plainest things, the darkest, the commonest things, the rarest.

I have had an amusing adventure — and made a friend.

This morning when I went to town for my marketing I met a man who was a Mason, an Oddfellow and an Elk, and who wore the evidences of his various memberships upon his coat. He asked me what lodge I belonged to, and he slapped me on the back in the heartiest manner, as though he had known me intimately for a long time. . . . I could not help feeling complimented — both complimented and abashed. For I am not a Mason, or an Oddfellow, or an Elk. When I told him so he seemed . . . surprised and disappointed.

"You ought to belong to one of our lodges," he said. "You'd be sure of having loyal friends wherever you go. . . . "You're just the sort of man," he said, "that we'd like to have in our lodge. I'd enjoy giving you the grip of fellowship." . . .

As I drove homeward this afternoon I could not help thinking of the Masons, the Oddfellows and the Elks — and curiously not without a sense of depression. I wondered if my friend . . . had found the pearl of great price that I have been looking for so long. For is not friendliness the thing of all things that is most pleasant in this world? Sometimes it has seemed to me that the faculty of reaching out and touching one's neighbour where he really lives is the greatest of human achievements. And it was with an indescribable depression that I wondered if these Masons and Oddfellows and Elks had in reality caught the Elusive Secret and confined it within the insurmountable and impenetrable walls of their mysteries, secrets, grips, passes, benefits.

"It must, indeed," I said to myself, "be a precious sort of fraternity that they choose to protect so sedulously."

I felt as though life contained something that I was not permitted to live. . . . So I jogged along feeling rather blue, marveling that those things which often seem so simple should be in reality so difficult.

The moment I passed the straggling outskirts of the town and came to the open road, the light and glow of the countryside came in upon me with a newness and sweetness impossible to describe. . . . I straightened up in my buggy and drew in a good breath. . . . "Why!" I exclaimed to myself, "I need not envy my friend's lodges. I myself belong to the greatest of all fraternal orders. I am a member of the Universal Brotherhood of Men." . . .

As I drove onward, . . . I saw a man walking in the road ahead of me. He was much bent over, and carried on his back a bag. When he heard me coming he stepped out of the road and stood silent, saving every unnecessary motion, as a weary man will. He neither looked around nor spoke, but waited for me to go by. He was weary past expectation. I stopped the mare.

"Get in, Brother," I said; "I am going your way."

He looked at me doubtfully; then, as I moved to one side, he let his bag roll off his back into his arms. I could see the swollen veins of his neck; his face had the drawn look of the man who bears burdens.

"Pretty heavy for your buggy," he remarked.

"Heavier for you," I replied.

So he put the bag in the back of my buggy and stepped in beside me diffidently.

"Pull up the lap robe," I said, "and be comfortable. . . . Aren't you the man who has taken the old Rucker farm?" I asked.

"I'm that man."

"I've been intending to drop in and see you," I said.

"Have you?" he asked eagerly.

"Yes," I said. "I live just across the hills from you, and I had a notion that we ought to be neighbourly—seeing that we belong to the same society."

His face, which had worn a look of set discouragement . . . had brightened up, but when I spoke of the society it clouded again.

"You must be mistaken," he said. "I'm not a Mason."

"No more am I," I said.

"Nor an Oddfellow."

"Nor I."

As I looked at the man I seemed to know all about him. . . . A man who in his time had seen many an open door, but who had found them all closed when he attempted to enter! If anyone ever needed the benefits of my fraternity, he was that man.

"What Society did you think I belonged to?" he asked. . . . "I haven't any money to pay into lodges and it don't seem's if a man could get acquainted and friendly without."

"Farming is rather lonely work sometimes, isn't it?" I observed.

"You bet it is," he responded. "You've been there yourself, haven't you?"

There may be such a thing as the friendship of prosperity; but surely it cannot be compared with the friendship of adversity. Men, stooping, come close together.

"But when I got to thinking it over," I said, "it suddenly occurred to me that I belonged to the greatest of all fraternities. And I recognized you instantly as a charter member."

He looked around at me expectantly, half laughing. I don't suppose he had so far forgotten his miseries for many a day.

"What's that?" he asked.

"The Universal Brotherhood of Men."

Well, we both laughed—and understood. After that, what a story he told me!—the story of a misplaced man on an unproductive farm. Is it not marvellous how full people are—all people—of humour, tragedy, passionate human longings, hopes, fears—if only you can unloosen the floodgates! (David Grayson, *Adventures in Friendship,* New York: Doubleday, Page & Company, 1922, pp. 1–16.)

Can the organization to which we belong, the one in which we claim membership, be recognized by our actions? Can we be identified as brothers and sisters, sons and daughters, in God's kingdom? Do our clubs ever separate us from our covenants?

It is easy to treat certain people kindly because we like them, for they are part of our group. But as true disciples of the Lord, we will endeavor to treat everyone kindly. As we do, we will find more and more people we like, including those whom we thought we might never like in the beginning. We will not experience in this mortal sphere the capacity to love as Christ loved, but in our feeble effort to make daily progress, the Lord will hear our earnest prayers, our desire to be a true disciple, and with his help we can participate in life-changing experiences for ourselves and for others.

Love has been defined as "the will to extend one's self for the purpose of nurturing one's own and another's spiritual growth." (M. Scott Peck, *The Road Less Traveled,* New York: Touchtone, 1978, p. 81.)

One time when I was speaking to an adult fireside, I felt impressed to share something concerning my love and appreciation for an individual struggling to overcome the devastating problem of alcoholism. Upon my return home, I received a letter from someone in that audience, a stranger until that night, and now a friend. A woman suffering from the effects of alcoholism in her own life wrote, "Since that Saturday night that I met you, I've been so filled with the Spirit, I have walked around for days now with a lump in my throat. For the first time in years I have prayed to my Father in Heaven, and I feel hope. I'm longing to come 'home.' I feel such an urgency to change. I've always felt like the last leaf on the tree, clinging for all it's worth, not courageous enough to let go and fall, afraid the fall will hurt. I hang on all alone. It's as though you reached out your hand and said, 'It's okay, let go. I'll be here. You're not alone.' This fall as I watch the golden leaves break loose and drift from their branches, I will think of you. Maybe someone else will regain their testimony because of your love and concern. Maybe they, like me, have found the courage to let go because a hand was there to hold."

If love can be expressed and felt between two people in an entire congregation, think what can happen when you express love to one another in small groups or just one to another. We need each other.

What will you do this year about love? Will this year be a retread, same old habits, liking some people, disliking others, ignoring or rejecting others? It is said that to ignore or to reject is even more devastating to people than to dislike them. Could you raise your voice to express a friendly hello to a fellow traveler who might be carrying a load on his back?

Each year since 1967, I have taken from my file a little statement to refresh my mind concerning the opportunities of a new year. May I share it with you:

> January . . . will this year be a retread—same old habits, same old ways, same old weaknesses, same old mistakes, same old heartaches, same old procrastinations? Or will this new year for you be a fresh and wonderful beginning-to-be-better kind of experience? . . . A little more like thee, Lord. A little more like thee! I would have . . . a heart more open to feel thy Spirit, to warm my brothers' needs, and sensitive enough to help fill them . . . a mind more receptive to know thy will, thy ways, thy purposes for all, and keen enough to respond . . . a self more ready to help in thy cause, to ease the burdens of my fellows, to calm the confusions in minds muddled by a world gone wrong, and pure enough to be the temple of my eternal spirit. (Marion D. Hanks and Elaine Cannon, "A Little More Like Thee, Lord," *Improvement Era,* January 1967, p. 34.)

How would it be and what would happen if we were to never withhold our love from our roommate, our neighbor, a parent, a brother, a sister, or a friend? Christ described how we should act: "Love your enemies, bless them that curse you, do good to them that hate you, and pray for them which despitefully use you, and persecute you." (Matthew 5:44.)

This year reach beyond your in-group and invite everyone in. And if you don't like someone now, act as if you do. This matter of loving others is not a manufactured feeling. If we love God, we ask what he would have us do and then we do it. We love others as he has loved us.

C. S. Lewis has given us great insight into what a Christian society is like. He said that it "is not going to arrive until most of us really want it: and we are not going to want it until we become fully Christian. I may repeat, 'Do as you would be done by' till I am black in the face, but I cannot really carry it out till

I love my neighbour as myself: and I cannot learn to love my neighbour as myself till I learn to love God: and I cannot learn to love God except by learning to obey Him. And so, as I warned you, we are driven on to something more inward—driven on from social matters to religious matters. For the longest way round is the shortest way home." (*Mere Christianity,* New York: Macmillan, 1960, pp. 82–83.)

Love and friendship are not a social matter. They are a deeply religious matter. Love does make the world go around. When we are striving to exert ourselves in the cause of spiritual growth for another, we discover that genuine love is self-replenishing and, in turn, nurtures our own spiritual growth.

Three-year-old Natalie and her little brother were in a quiet conversation. Their mother observed a tender moment between them as Natalie took her brother's hand and placed it over her heart, then asked, "Can you feel Jesus in there? You know Jesus is in your heart." Natalie expressed what Alma taught: "And this I know, because the Lord hath said he dwelleth not in unholy temples, but in the hearts of the righteous doth he dwell." (Alma 34:36.)

When the Lima Temple in Peru was nearing completion in 1985, I watched a handful of true disciples, many of them child-like in their faith, feeling the Spirit of Jesus in their hearts as they sacrificed much, living in poverty, in a spirit of love of one another, sharing all that they had in full anticipation of the blessings promised in the temple. Free from pride and undistracted by the material things of the world, they reached out in love one to another as brothers and sisters, as Latter-day Saints.

As I prepared to leave these people, amid hugs and tears and love, they presented me with a small pillow about four inches square that they had made from rather worn material, filled with sawdust gathered from the temple site. It was a gift of love, more precious to me than many expensive items I have in my possession. Often it is the little things that become most precious in expressing love. Emily Dickinson wrote, "Sometimes when I consider the tremendous consequences from little things . . . a chance word . . . a tap on the shoulder or a wink of an eye, I am tempted to think there are no little things."

The Prophet Joseph Smith taught, "Nothing is so much calculated to lead people to forsake sin as to take them by the hand, and watch over them with tenderness. When persons manifest the least kindness and love to me, O what power it has over my mind, while the opposite course has a tendency to harrow up all the harsh feelings and depress the human mind." (*Teachings of the Prophet Joseph Smith,* p. 240.)

Mother Teresa has said, "We wait impatiently for the paradise where God is, but we have it in our power to be in paradise with Him, right now; being happy with Him means: To love as He loves. To help as He helps. To give as He gives. To serve as He serves." (*Love: A Fruit Always in Season,* San Francisco: Ignatius Press, 1987, p. 110.)

Can we—will we—reach out and extend our love? What would happen if each of us were to strive to feel and express greater love in our families this year than ever before? What can we do to bring greater feelings of love into our circle of influence? Mother Teresa said, "It is not how much we do but the love we give that really matters." The Lord, through the Prophet Joseph Smith, taught us, "No one can assist in this work except he shall be humble and full of love." (D&C 12:8.)

What would happen if each of us were to give up selfish, petty, uncharitable feelings and attitudes, criticism, and negative comments, and replace them with sincere concern, kindness, and love? What would happen if each of us had the courage and the love required to take Jesus at his word? What if, as we plan our activities, rather than asking "What shall we do?" we were to ask "What do we want to have happen?" And if, into our minds, we heard the words "Bring souls unto Christ," what do you think might happen? Some people are doing this, and others of us are talking and thinking about it and thinking that someday we will.

I have a friend I would like to tell you about. This woman, who never married, has many friends but few family members—

no parents, brothers, or sisters. On the little piece of property that she purchased through her hard labors some years ago, she built a small home.

Not long ago I extended an invitation for Christmas to this dear sister. She responded, "Thank you. I appreciate your invitation, but I think I'll go where I did last year, down to the homeless-shelter soup kitchen where I can do some good. That experience brings me such joy. I do so little, and yet I always come home with a soft, warm glow and feel His presence in my home. I'm not alone." Then she explained, "It is a grand feeling. Nothing else makes me feel quite this way."

There was a light in her eye and a smile on her face as she spoke of giving hope. How exciting life could become if we were to lose ourselves and in turn find our real selves by extending love beyond our immediate circle of friends.

Love is the foundation for righteousness, salvation, and peace. President Spencer W. Kimball taught, "The Lord does hear and answer our prayers, but He usually answers them through someone else." ("Small Acts of Service," *Ensign*, December 1974, p. 5.) Will you or I be that someone else? One of the sure signs that a person has accepted the gift of the Savior's atonement is that person's ability to love. An acknowledgment of his love for us makes us more sensitive, more gracious, more anxious to reach out. The Savior describes the blessings that come to those who catch this message:

> Then shall the King say unto them on his right hand, Come, ye blessed of my Father, inherit the kingdom prepared for you from the foundation of the world:
> For I was an hungred, and ye gave me meat: I was thirsty, and ye gave me drink: I was a stranger, and ye took me in:
> Naked, and ye clothed me: I was sick, and ye visited me: I was in prison, and ye came unto me.
> Then shall the righteous answer him, saying, Lord, when saw we thee an hungred, and fed thee? or thirsty, and gave thee drink?
> When saw we thee a stranger, and took thee in? or naked, and clothed thee?

Or when saw we thee sick, or in prison, and came unto thee?

And the King shall answer and say unto them, Verily I say unto you, Inasmuch as ye have done it unto one of the least of these my brethren, ye have done it unto me. (Matthew 25:34–40.)

We need not wait for Valentine's Day or any other special day to show love. We can experience a bit of heaven every day when our hearts reach out in love to one another. God help us to make the world go around and do our part as we pray, "Thy kingdom come. Thy will be done, on earth as it is in heaven." (Matthew 6:10.)

CHAPTER 3

With Faith,
Hope, and Charity

I n my family room by the old-fashioned rocker is a large knitting basket. It has been there for several years. In the basket
are some bright balls of yarn along with several balls of black
yarn. Some unused knitting needles poking through the yarn
appear to be in the same position they were the day they were
taken from the packages and placed there with eagerness and
great anticipation. Today the basket of yarn serves as a decorator
piece and gives a homey look to the room.

When I purchased the yarn many years ago, I had a different
purpose in mind. I was going to make a beautiful afghan like
one I had seen in a friend's home. I borrowed the pattern from
her, then purchased the needles and the yarn with good intentions, but as yet I do not have an afghan. While there are great
possibilities awaiting in that basket, the probability of making
an afghan decreases each year. My enthusiasm and vision for
what I once planned to do has diminished, faded into the background, pushed aside by other interests. What I see now is just
a colorful basket of yarn that makes a nice accent piece beside
a rocker. An afghan would be nice, but it certainly isn't essential,
and the fact that other things have crowded in to take my attention and interest is of little concern. However, there are some
things that are a concern, some things that must not be left in
the basket unattended, if I am to experience the rewards and
the marvelous possibilities of what can be.

Afghans are made, goals are reached, dreams are realized,

31

and victories are won by diligence, determination, and persistent desire—not as a single event, but through a steady, forward movement with our eye ever on the goal. We each have within our basket, so to speak, within our souls, threads of faith, threads of hope, threads of charity.

We did not come to this earth to gain faith, hope, or charity. We brought these characteristics of a divine nature with us to be developed through our daily experiences. But until these eternal principles become a part of our daily lives, they will lie dormant within, unused, undeveloped, and no more valuable than the bright balls of yarn in my sewing basket.

With the divine attributes of faith, hope, and charity nurtured daily, we not only witness miracles, but we also participate in them. The miracle takes place as we reach out to others; and then, in turn, a change takes place within us—a miracle within us, the mighty change of heart of which Alma spoke, in describing what happened when Abinadi preached to the Nephites: "A mighty change was also wrought in their hearts, and they humbled themselves and put their trust in the true and living God." (Alma 5:13.)

Once we begin to weave these great eternal principles into our daily lives, we realize we no longer yearn to have faith. We have faith, and we desire to increase in faith from day to day. We no longer yearn for hope; we have hope, and we desire to increase in hope from day to day. We no longer yearn for charity; we have charity, and we desire to increase in charity from day to day. This miracle from within begins to be revealed in our countenances. We learn to view this life from the perspective of eternity and imagine we can hear the voice of the Lord, saying, "Come unto me ye blessed, for behold, your works have been the works of righteousness upon the face of the earth." (Alma 5:16.) Just as a ball of yarn does not make an afghan, so faith without works is dead. We must do our part.

In *The Miracle of Forgiveness,* President Spencer W. Kimball quoted Oliver Wendell Holmes, who said, "Many people die with their music still in them. Why is this so? Too often it is because they are always getting ready to live. Before they know it, time runs out." He noted also that Tagore expressed a similar thought: "I have spent my days stringing and unstringing my instrument, while the song I came to sing remains unsung." After quoting these two thoughts, President Kimball commented, "Let us get our instruments tightly strung and our melodies sweetly sung." (Salt Lake City: Bookcraft, 1969, pp. 16–17.)

On those occasions when faith wanes, hope wavers, and charity seems like something for another day, perhaps an increased awareness of what encumbers the weaving, slows the progress, and inhibits our growth can serve as a warning to us. It has to do with time — our limited time and our sense of pressure to do it all, all at once.

William James, sometimes referred to as the father of psychology, said, "Neither the nature nor the amount of our work is accountable for the frequency and severity of our breakdowns, but their cause lies rather in those observed feelings of hurry and having no time, breathless tension and anxiety, the lack of inner harmony and ease."

One might thoughtlessly say, "If I just had enough faith, I would take time for spiritual things." The result of that thinking does not increase one's faith or one's time. On the other hand, if we set priorities that require setting, and set aside some things for a season, we will find that in the process we will once again hear the squeaks in the swing and the whisperings of the Spirit.

When I was a child growing up on the prairie in Alberta, Canada, we had some rather severe winters. My mother had a little grocery store, and early each morning I would go out with my father to kindle a fire in the old coal stove and try to get the place warm before customers began to come. One morning while sitting on a bench watching my father lay the kindling for the fire, I learned a great lesson that I reflect on frequently. He explained, as he carefully put paper and kindling wood and larger pieces of wood into the stove, "Ardie, my dear, you can stand in front of this stove for a long time waiting for heat, and it will never come. You must put the wood in first and then the heat will come. Some people are like a coal stove. They want to have the heat first, and then they'll put in the wood. They want the blessings, and then they will have faith. You must place the wood in with faith and then the heat will come."

I have discovered over the years that when we do our part, we not only experience the warmth, the heat, the security, and the peace, but we are also privileged to witness miracles and even participate in them. We witness miracles that are performed not by our own strength or resources, but—like the heat from the old coal stove—by the power of God added to our own meager efforts, diligence, persistence, and faith. We are reminded in Ether, "Dispute not because ye see not, for ye receive no witness until after the trial of your faith." (Ether 12:6.)

And how long must we sustain the trial of our faith before the miracle occurs? That trial may last days or months or even years. The weaving occurs ever so carefully, day by day, but only if we make time. Our time is our life, and whatever it is we are doing with our time, we are paying for it with our life. The challenge of mortality is to manage our time in such a way that what we spend it on is worth our life. It is the threads of faith, of hope, and of charity that are worthy of giving our time to, our life to. And in the process, over a period of time, a miracle takes place.

You remember the story of the man blind from birth who waited in darkness until the Savior ministered unto him. We read that the Savior "spat on the ground, and made clay of the spittle, and he anointed the eyes of the blind man with the clay." He then commanded the man to "go, wash in the pool of Siloam." As quickly as the blind man washed his eyes with the water as commanded, he could see. He was brought out of darkness into the light—the light given him by the Lord Jesus Christ.

It was a miracle, the people said. Some might have referred to it as an instant miracle, but others would recognize it as the final act of the miracle a long time in the making. Who can

34

measure the spiritual growth that might have taken place in the blind man during the days, the months, and the years of darkness while he was waiting upon the Lord? The recorded account does not indicate how long he suffered. We do know that when the Lord reached out to bless him, the man was ready to receive and bear testimony of the miracle. He said, "A man that is called Jesus made clay, and anointed mine eyes, and said unto me, Go to the pool of Siloam, and wash: and I went and washed, and I received sight." A transformation had taken place. His faith was tried and tested, and one day he came out of the darkness into the light. (John 9:6–7, 11.)

Dr. Truman G. Madsen has written: "Again and again we participate in programs designed to change behavior. Within limits they have wholesome and lasting effects, but the announced intent of Christ in the transformation of man and family is far more inclusive. It is to change behavior, to change our souls in nature, in inclination, in desire. That is like replacing the tissues and bones of a person while he is still alive. It is like rebuilding a ship at sea. But again and again, we see the process at work. Personality is illuminated and purified through the renovating powers of the gospel. We see hopeless problems diminished." (*Marriage and Family: Gospel Insights,* Salt Lake City: Bookcraft, 1983, p. 75.)

The first of the Young Women Values is Faith. There is great power in this statement: "I am a daughter of a Heavenly Father who loves me, and I will have faith in his eternal plan, which centers in Jesus Christ, my Savior."

It is with faith in that eternal plan and knowing of our identity, knowing that God is our Father and we are indeed his children, that our faith is strong and hope removes from our path obstacles that otherwise seem insurmountable.

Hope is like a bridge that links faith and charity. It is an outgrowth of faith. Hope is just not a wish. It is the expectation of the fulfillment of a promise. It comes from a sacred covenant made with the Lord.

The development of hope is a process, not an event. Just as

the bright colors of the yarn taken from my basket, when gradually woven together according to the pattern, can become an afghan, so the experiences in our daily lives can evolve in a miraculous way according to the pattern, the plan of salvation. Like the blind man, we are touched by the hand of God, and in due time we begin to see. We see with an eye of faith full of hope. Faith is to hope for things which are not seen, but which are true.

Hope comes from the sure conviction that when we have done our very best, the Savior, by the grace of God, will do the rest. That is an expectation that we can depend on. One of the biggest obstacles to acquiring and maintaining hope is that we must deal with the reality of mortality. While struggling with that distance between where we are and where we desire to be as we move toward our ultimate goal of exaltation, we so often fall short. Our hope can be shattered until we begin to understand that life is a journey, and our progress comes as we learn to understand the very purpose of life, including the need for suffering, setbacks, trials, and tests. The Prophet Joseph Smith had one of his greatest experiences at one of the darkest times of his life. While he was confined, in anguish and sorrow, within the walls of the jail in Liberty, Missouri, there came a great light and an abiding revelation: "Fear not what man can do, for God shall be with you forever and ever." (D&C 122:9.)

God, our Eternal Father, lives. He is kind; he is loving; he is our Eternal Parent; he is perfect. We are not perfect. We are in this life to be tried and to be tested.

Life on this sphere is what we call mortality and represents the second phase of our life's experiences. One day we will leave this mortal life and live in a world with other spirit beings, eagerly anticipating our resurrection. We live, we die, we move on, but we do not all progress at the same rate, and often the most readily apparent progress is not the most significant. Time-consuming detours can slow progress and eventually destroy hope. Our hope increases as we learn to select some things and leave other, less important, things behind. We each have our own basket of things we treasure. In our immaturity, we may go after those things that give us immediate and temporary pleasure, but gradually we begin to value many things in a much different light.

Hope comes as we learn to look at the struggles and even the suffering of this life as a time of learning and progress. We read of our Savior: "Though he were a Son, yet learned he obedience by the things which he suffered." (Hebrews 5:8.) Often faith wavers and weakens when we are focusing on our weaknesses and our inadequacies, or, while reviewing the accomplishments and seeming success of others, we evaluate ourselves and come up short. It would be wise for us to follow the counsel of the old farmer who, when asked how he was doing, simply responded, "I am better than I was, but I ain't as good as I'm going to be." That, I believe, reflects an attitude of hope.

Each day of our life, each week, our hope will increase as we learn to focus on the positives and get rid of the thoughts and feelings that destroy our faith and our hope.

In many locales throughout the world, municipal workers come to our homes each week to collect the garbage we have accumulated during the preceding seven days. Every Sunday we can also get rid of the mental and emotional garbage that may have accumulated during the week. President Marion G. Romney explained: "There is a doctrine abroad in the world today which teaches that the physical emblems of the sacrament are transformed into the flesh and blood of Jesus. We do not teach such a doctrine, for we know that any transformation which comes from the administration of the sacrament takes place in the souls of those who understandingly partake of it. It is the participating individuals who are affected, and they are affected in a most marvelous way, for they are given the Spirit of the Lord to be with them." (*Conference Report*, April 1946, p. 40.) Every Sunday starts a new week. Every hour starts a new set of minutes. Our God, our Father, is in the heavens, but that's not far away. He's near us.

We must not let our weaknesses weaken our hope. The

Savior has told us, "If men come unto me I will show unto them their weakness. I give unto men weakness that they may be humble; and my grace is sufficient for all men that humble themselves before me; for if they humble themselves before me, and have faith in me, then will I make weak things become strong unto them." (Ether 12:27.)

I don't believe the Lord gives us our weaknesses. He gives us our *weakness*, and a better understanding of that gives us hope. We read in Jacob, "Nevertheless, the Lord God showeth us our weakness that we may know that it is by his grace, and his great condescensions unto the children of men, that we have power to do these things." (Jacob 4:7.) Our weakness is that we are mortal, and with God's help we can become immortal and have eternal life.

The gift of hope is illustrated by the Lord's blessings to Alma and his followers when they were in bondage and were carrying heavy burdens. Alma and his people pled with the Lord with enough hope and enough faith that "the burdens which were laid upon [them] were made light; yea, the Lord did strengthen them that they could bear up their burdens with ease, and that they did submit cheerfully and with patience to all the will of the Lord. And it came to pass that so great was their faith and their patience that the voice of the Lord came unto them again, saying: Be of good comfort, for on the morrow I will deliver you out of bondage." (Mosiah 24:15–16.)

When we diligently strive to do our very best, withholding nothing, we come to better understand that through the grace of God we have reason to hope.

In the Bible Dictionary we read that grace "is an enabling power that allows men and women to lay hold on eternal life and exaltation." Paul, speaking to the Romans, helps us understand this process: "Therefore being justified by faith, we have peace with God through our Lord Jesus Christ: by whom also we have access by faith into this grace [enabling power] wherein we stand, and rejoice in hope of the glory of God. And not only so, but we glory in tribulations also: knowing that tribulation worketh patience; and patience, experience; and experience, hope: and hope maketh not ashamed; because the love of God is shed abroad in our hearts by the Holy Ghost which is given unto us." (Romans 5:1–5.)

It is not God's plan that we should be perfect before we can experience hope. It is in our imperfections and our dependency upon God that we seek and find our hope. "God commendeth his love toward us, in that, while we were yet sinners, Christ died for us." (Romans 5:8.)

Early one rainy morning, I walked along the boulevard on my regular path before the day began. In thoughtful meditation, with a multitude of responsibilities that seemed to extend far beyond my ability, I began enumerating in my mind a list of my inadequacies and weaknesses. That activity, by the way, is like priming a pump. If you can get started with just a little water and keep pumping, the flow of water will continue with hardly any effort and will fill bucket after bucket. And so it was. I soon began focusing on all the things that I don't know that I would like to know. I don't know how to use the computer very well, I don't know mathematics, I don't know how to sing, I can't spell, and on and on. The list is endless and even ridiculous once one begins such a useless, unsettling activity. Finally, in the quiet of that early morning, as the gentle rain washed the sidewalk, it was as though the windows of heaven opened and poured out living water upon my head in one brief message. Like a separation of the clouds with the sun coming through, my whole soul was cleansed of the worries for the things I don't know and filled with this sure conviction: "I know that my Redeemer lives." And then like a whisper came the words into my mind, "That is enough."

We read in Ether, "I also remember that thou hast said that thou hast prepared a house for man, yea, even among the mansions of thy Father, in which man might have a more excellent hope; wherefore man must hope, or he cannot receive an inheritance in the place which thou hast prepared. . . . And now I know that this love which thou hast had for the children of men is charity; wherefore, except men shall have charity they cannot inherit that place which thou hast prepared in the mansions of thy Father." (Ether 12:32, 34.)

The pure love of Christ, that charity of which we speak, is a golden thread woven through the tapestry of our daily lives. It is the outgrowth of faith and hope. It is the thread that ties us, binds us, and seals us to our Father. The Lord gave us an example of this golden thread in his illustration of the Good Samaritan. We read of a lawyer who asked the Master what he should do to inherit eternal life. And the Lord answered, "Thou shalt love the Lord thy God with all thy heart, and with all thy soul, and with all thy strength, and with all thy mind; and thy neighbour as thyself." (Luke 10:27.)

At the conclusion of Mormon's sermon on faith, hope, and charity, we read, "Charity is the pure love of Christ, and it endureth forever; and whoso is found possessed of it at the last day, it shall be well with him. Wherefore, my beloved brethren, pray unto the Father with all the energy of heart, that ye may be filled with this love, which he hath bestowed upon all who are true followers of his Son, Jesus Christ; that ye may become the sons of God; that when he shall appear we shall be like him, for we shall see him as he is; that we may have this hope; that we may be purified even as he is pure." (Moroni 7:47–48.)

We cannot develop charity on our own. When we do our very best, our Savior, through the grace of God, his enabling power, will do the rest.

What hope can come to us when we remember that God is our Father and we are his children! As Ether explains, "Whoso believeth in God might with surety hope for a better world, yea, even a place at the right hand of God, which hope cometh of faith, maketh an anchor to the souls of men, which would make them sure and steadfast, always abounding in good works, being led to glorify God." (Ether 12:4.)

Should I determine to pick up the needles and the colorful yarn from my knitting basket and carefully follow the pattern written in detail with illustrations, one day I would have an afghan. But left unattended with only good intentions set aside indefinitely, the potential of what might be will never be realized. The pattern has been provided for us in the Book of Mormon:

> And again, my beloved brethren, I would speak unto you concerning hope. How is it that ye can attain unto faith, save ye shall have hope? And what is it that ye shall hope for? Behold I say unto you that ye shall have hope through the atonement of Christ and the power of his resurrection, to be raised unto life eternal, and this because of your faith in him according to the promise.
>
> Wherefore, if a man have faith he must needs have hope; for without faith there cannot be any hope.
>
> And again, behold I say unto you that he cannot have faith and hope, save he shall be meek, and lowly of heart. If so, his faith and hope is vain, for none is acceptable before God, save the meek and lowly in heart; and if a man be meek and lowly in heart, and confesses by the power of the Holy Ghost that Jesus is the Christ, he must needs have charity; for if he have not charity he is nothing; wherefore he must needs have charity.
>
> And charity suffereth long, and is kind, and envieth not, and is not puffed up, seeketh not her own, is not easily provoked, thinketh no evil, and rejoiceth not in iniquity but rejoiceth in the truth, beareth all things, believeth all things, hopeth all things, endureth all things. (Moroni 7:40–45.)

I bear testimony that as we strive to weave threads of faith, hope, and charity into our lives, there will be times when the process is slow. We will be tried and tested. But when we come offering a broken heart and a contrite spirit, we will be conscious of the nearness of our Father in heaven, and we will feel charity for all our Father's children.

The Prophet Joseph Smith taught: "The nearer we get to our Heavenly Father, the more we are disposed to look with compassion on perishing souls: we feel that we want to take them upon our shoulders, and cast their sins behind our backs." (*Teachings of the Prophet Joseph Smith*, p. 241.)

My niece Shelly, while serving a mission in New Zealand,

expressed it this way in a letter: "I want to be worthy of the Spirit to help these people have the best chance of hearing the gospel. I have never worked harder or cared more about people. I have never prayed so hard for investigators. The Lord truly performs miracles. I love having FAITH! We love our investigators and want to obey all the rules so that when we pray for them, it will work."

When we do our part, the pure love of Christ will fill our souls and we will come rejoicing.

CHAPTER 4

You Can Do It
If You Have a Mind To

It was like turning a page in a favorite old picture book with a story that began "Once upon a time . . . " Sister Verna Hill, seventy-seven years of age, stood in the driveway of her home wearing a bright red dress with white polka dots and her arm outstretched in welcome. Her white hair framed a truly radiant countenance.

"Do come in and sit down," Sister Hill said, motioning toward one of her two front rooms. As I walked in, I glanced around in an attempt to see and feel, at least in part, the charm of this humble home where Sister Hill lived alone. I observed a magnificent display of handiwork: colorful afghans, delicate and intricate designs captured through the art of tatting, and cutwork of the finest quality. A multitude of pictures of loved ones, placed here and there, added to the warmth and love that filled the old home. I sat on the carpet by her footstool while she leaned back in her big chair and, like turning the pages in a book, permitted me to peek inside her life.

"Well, it was like this," she began, reaching back over the years in time, yet with the vividness of just yesterday. "I had the misfortune of losing my parents when I was only twelve years of age. My mother died just before Christmas, and the following Thanksgiving my father had a heart attack and died in his chair." She was reflective a moment, then continued her story. "I called a Brother Blood, who was our closest neighbor.

He and his dear wife, Minnie, were so good to me. They treated me like their very own."

Verna Hill was the youngest of eleven children and was the only one left at home at the time of her parents' death. She wanted to finish the eighth grade before going to Nevada to live with a brother, so she found work to support herself. "I worked for a lady who had a new baby, and I did housework for my room and board," she explained.

After the eighth grade, Sister Hill did not have the benefit of any additional formal education. She moved to a ranch in Nevada with her brother, whose wife was in the hospital, and for the next three months she cooked for eighteen men who worked in the hay fields.

"Well, I got very, very homesick," she recalled, "so I decided to move to another ranch at Winnemucca, where I could be with my older brother. He said, 'I want you to come and stay with me.'" He agreed to meet her at the hotel in Winnemucca. When this young girl, now only thirteen, got out of the stagecoach after her long ride, the hotel manager met her and said, "Your brother has been called to Elko for a few days, but your room and board are paid for."

After a brief stay in Winnemucca, she decided to move on. "I could have gone and lived with my sisters," she told me, "but they had their families, and I knew the time had come I was going to have to support myself."

This woman, in the face of great difficulties, learned to make the best of every situation. She developed the will to win, to take life as it comes and to make something beautiful out of it. "You can't always choose or change circumstances," she said now, reaching over and patting my hand as if to make sure I understood. "But how you accept them and how you feel about them is up to you."

While doing housework for others and learning to cook and sew, she took every opportunity to develop her skills. "You know," she said, smiling confidently, "there isn't any kind of handwork I can't do."

"I understand that you have won prizes for your cooking and that you are always cooking special dishes for your neighbors and family and give your handwork away," I commented.

With a twinkle in her eyes, she responded, "Well, I don't like bragging, you know, but I just love to give service. I've done it all my life and I enjoy it. So I cook and I sew, and I do whatever I can."

This seemed like a good opportunity to inquire about the piano and organ in her modest home. "Do you play?" I asked.

"Oh, I'm no professional," she admitted. "I only had six lessons before my mother died, but I can figure it out. It just comes to me because I have determined that I'm going to do it. I've been a ward organist for years."

Returning to her story, Sister Hill admitted that she married very young. She and her husband, Leo, worked side by side. Together they mowed and hauled hay and raked it. They dug up potatoes, picked tomatoes, and hoed beets and corn. Sister Hill also drove the tractor and the truck. She told of coming in dead tired, but after a bath and supper, she would pick up some handwork. "And you know," she said, "before long I would forget about being tired. Just because your body is tired that's no need for your mind and hands to have to rest. If I sit down to rest without my handwork, I'd go to sleep when I could be doing something."

Just three days after her second daughter was born, the bishop and his counselors came to visit. "I thought they'd come to see me and the baby, but they didn't," she told me. "They came to see Leo. They wanted him to go on a mission. Leo and I talked about it and decided if that was what the Lord wanted, I'd get along."

While her young husband was away, Sister Hill opened up a dress shop in Layton, Utah, where they had settled. She bought two machines, a regular one and a hemstitcher. "I bought this hemstitching machine and then I learned how to use it—and I'm still using it," she said. "I never had a formal education, but ladies still come for me to teach them."

45

She pointed to a collection of pictures nearby. "See that young man's picture on the TV? I'm real proud of him." Her voice was tender and a little emotional as she recalled, "That boy's mother lost her life when she was seven months pregnant with him. Her husband was serving his country in Germany. After forty-one days I brought that baby home from the hospital. He was an awful sight. His skin was just like paper. He was so sick, I cried and cried all night. My husband said, 'Mama, you can't keep that baby if you're going to be so upset.' We called the doctor and he said, 'You'll never raise that baby.' I said, 'Well, I'm going to give him the best care I can.' I just oiled that baby three or four times a day for six months. You wouldn't believe how well he is now." Looking again at his picture on the TV, she repeated, "I'm really proud of him."

She drew my attention to a picture on the wall, of a little home where her husband was born, located just behind her present home. "There was a man came to work for my husband years ago," she explained. "He had no folks so we took him in and he worked for us. We treated him like he was ours. He meant a lot to us. He lived in that little house for fifty-three years, and when he died we saw to it that he had a proper burial."

She got up from her chair, and I followed her to view her precious treasures more closely. Picking up one picture, she said, "When I was president of the Relief Society, a young mother was left with seven children. I took them under my wing and became their adopted grandmother. Those kids are married now and come to visit me with their children. One of them was here last night. He came by to fix my cooler."

She picked up another picture. "This boy came to live with me for a time," she said. "I made him acquainted with a young girl in our ward and they got married. They wanted me to stand in their reception line. I said, 'Oh, no,' but they insisted." Putting his picture back in its special place, she commented with pride, "He's a fine musician."

Sister Hill returned to her chair. Without words to express

the love that poured from the heart of this saintly woman, I asked, "How did you get this great spirit of wanting to give and serve and care so much and so deeply about people?"

Almost as if waiting for that question, she replied, "I'm going to tell you just how we learn to help others. My daddy used to always say, 'You can't take anything with you—only what you give away.' And that has stayed with me."

"Now that you're alone without your companion, how do you keep up your radiant and enthusiastic attitude of serving and caring?" I asked.

Leaning forward in her chair she pondered a moment, then said quietly, "I've missed Daddy. You have hard times." Tears filled her eyes. "But I've learned to make the best of things." Her smile returned with her determination, and she continued, "Well, dear, I'm going to tell you how I do it. I made up my mind you can't do any good staying home grieving. My husband was always active, and I know he is progressing now, and he wouldn't be very happy with me if he knew I was just staying home, 'cause it doesn't do you any good. You've got to look ahead to tomorrow instead of just for today and keep going."

Inspired by her energy I inquired further, "But where do you get your strength?"

As if surprised by this question, she responded very matter-of-factly. "From the Lord. You just have to depend on Him. Some nights when I get ready for bed and I think I can't stand it alone, after I kneel down and have my prayers, that comforting influence comes over me and I'm not nervous anymore because I know somebody is watching over me and guiding me."

"Do you ever get tired?"

"Oh, yes, I get tired," she confessed, "but then I don't let it get the best of me. You know what I mean. I got up at five o'clock this morning and I went out to water my garden. I can work and work and be so tired I can't go another minute; then I'll sit down and pick up some handwork, and the first thing you know I forget about being tired."

I asked her about her philosophy of life. With this she giggled

47

in a delightfully girlish manner. "Well," she said, "just work, work, work. I'm proud of my life. I haven't wasted any time. You gotta keep goin', haven't you?" Then, as if turning to the last page of a wonderful story, she closed with these penetrating words: "You can do it if you have a mind to."

Leaving her home, I carried with me the secrets to happiness and a beautiful handmade pillow under my arm.

CHAPTER 5

The Treasure We
Will Take with us

Her life-long dream had turned into what now seemed like a nightmare. During the long, hot summer days of picking potatoes and cucumbers, Alice had envisioned herself walking across the campus as a student at Brigham Young University. It was the goal that had kept her going when she would otherwise have given up. Her determination had brought her to BYU for fall semester. And now the frustration, the pressure, the anguish that she faced seemed more like a nightmare than a reward for such effort. She hadn't planned it this way. In fact, after arriving she had hardly planned at all.

Alice was one of the students in my class. Somehow she hadn't realized the big difference between going to school and learning. She found the social side of college life more enticing than studying and learning. The urgency of preparing for her final exam hit her only after the opportunity for preparation had almost passed. It all seemed like a nightmare now. She must not fail, but she was unprepared. She had not committed herself to an education; she was just going to school. She remembered people asking her back home, "What do you want to be when you grow up?" Growing up had seemed so far away until this day. Now she was searching for the answer to that question, not for them but for herself. What did she want to do with her life and how did an education fit in?

We must all face that question eventually if we are to be responsible for our lives. When we find the answer, we have a sense of what we want to learn or what kind of job we may someday have or how we can become a better mother and wife, because of our education. We catch a glimpse of a bigger picture—a purpose, a destination, a course of action for this life that determines what we can become through the eternities. It's when we catch even a glimpse of the excitement, the benefits, the opportunities, the richness of life that an education can provide, that the discipline required to study becomes a small price to pay.

With our eye toward eternity, education is the treasure we will take with us and will give us so much the advantage in the world to come. (D&C 130:18:19.) And for today, it can open doors to opportunities that would otherwise be closed tight. Nephi writes, "To be learned is good if they hearken unto the counsels of God." (2 Nephi 9:29.) If we lack wisdom we are to ask, and when we seek diligently we will know the truth. And the truth shall make us free (John 8:32)—free to make wise choices; free to experience life with ever-changing, wonderful, new horizons; free to speak up and speak out for what is right; free to influence those who are seeking truth; free to prepare in the time of youth for a rich and rewarding lifetime; free to hold on to the love of learning our whole life long, making every day more zestful.

Sister Camilla Kimball said, "What we must be concerned with is preparation for life, and that preparation is continuing education. Whether it is to earn a living or to rear a family, men and women both need to have the knowledge that enhances their natural talents." (Address at Brigham Young University, March 9, 1982.) Preparation for life is for young women who marry and those who may never marry. It is for women who will have children to help educate and others who will not. It is for women who will need to support themselves and their children at some time in their lives.

For some of us, this may mean going to college or a trade school. To others, it may mean home study. To all of us, it means looking at the longterm goal of making education a lifelong process, not just a two- or four-year event after high school called "higher education."

One might ask, does pursuing an education contradict our goal to marry and have a family? Definitely not! We need to be educated for our families as well as ourselves!

With all the contradiction and confusing voices, we are going to need our own clear direction more than ever before. A woman should always keep the goal of marriage and family foremost in the choices she makes. But she must also be prepared for other rich and wonderful experiences in building the kingdom.

A woman who is now a mother of eleven children dreamed in college of the lights of the stage, while taking classes in philosophy, economics, and political science and majoring in theater. Now she is on her own stage performing magnificently well. She has chosen to enrich, protect, and guard the home. This past summer she and another Mormon woman ran a campaign from their homes and were elected as two of four delegates to help choose a new leader for a political party. These same women later organized a rally in the city park on an issue they felt strongly would negatively affect life in their province in Canada.

I asked this sister how she manages to be so influential. "You have to know parliamentary procedure in public meetings," she replied. "If you do, you can safeguard democracy and your home by using the rules effectively."

"When and where does one learn these rules?" I asked.

She laughed and said, "Last night at supper, it went like this":

Sarah: "Honorable chairman, the soup is good."

Chairman: "Can I have a motion to that effect?"

Sharon: "I move that we go on record stating the soup is good."

Chairman: "Could I have a second?" Seconded. "Any discussion?"

Amy: "It's too spicy."

Chairman: "We will proceed to vote."

The results of the dinner: The soup passed. The jam passed

unanimously. And the motion in favor of the water was tabled for another time pending further investigation.

A mother who is well educated can help instill that same enthusiasm for learning in her children.

Classes in home economics and child development and family relations can help strengthen our families. And so can teaching and nursing, law and debate, political science, engineering, medicine, history, communications, and even statistics.

The question has been asked, if a woman is trained in such broad areas, will she be lured away from the home? In many ways, her education can strengthen her home. Down the road, higher education may give her more opportunity to be with her family, to set her own working hours, to have the know-how to go into business, to prepare her to meet the economic needs of her family if she must become the provider. Knowledge and intelligence are tools that can be used in righteousness or unrighteousness. Proper use can help us better protect and guard our homes.

Those who have a choice will be found protecting and guarding their families on the home front by the hearth. Others will be in foreign fields on occasion, working to keep the enemy away from our doors. Those fields may include participation in the PTA, in political parties, in civic organizations, and in various professions. Whether we are married or unmarried, with many children or none, education is important and is available right within the walls of our homes. No one needs to be deprived. We need to educate ourselves and prepare to defend our values and be a strong influence for righteousness.

When Queen Esther of the Old Testament was placed in the position to save the Jews in Persia from being put to death by appealing to her husband the king, her uncle Mordecai said to her, "Who knoweth whether thou art come to the kingdom for such a time as this?" (Esther 4:14.) Just as Esther was in the palace of the king to help her people, each of us have important things to accomplish, many of them established before we came to this earth.

President George Q. Cannon wrote, "God has chosen us out of the world and has given us a great mission. I do not entertain a doubt myself but that we were selected and fore-ordained for the mission before the world was, that we had our parts allotted to us in this mortal state of existence as our Savior had His assigned to Him." (*Gospel Truth,* Salt Lake City: Deseret Book, 1974, p. 18.)

As we seek to know the Lord's will and choose to carry it out, he will be there to guide us, to love us, to watch over us, to help us progress and learn. And because of our much learning, there will be many opportunities when our influence, our wisdom, our voice, and our vote will make the difference—not on whether the soup passes, but whether righteousness is defended.

What we become eventually will be what we prepare for now.

THE LIGHT WITHIN

CHAPTER 6

Who Lights the "Y"?

The crowds were gathering on the quad at Brigham Young University on October 8, 1991. The occasion was a Founder's Day celebration, held at the beginning of the annual homecoming festivities. People from far and wide were returning home for this special event. The air was filled with music as the band played familiar songs, awakening treasured memories for the older guests and generating excitement and enthusiasm for the current student body, while anxious hopes welled up in the hearts of those not yet college age.

Hovering over the entire assemblage like a sentinel keeping watch over the activities, the large block Y lay strong and secure on the side of the majestic mountain. That block Y had been there for as long as any of us could remember. It served as a marker whether one approached the campus by air or on the highway, and for the students walking to and from classes in summer, fall, winter, and spring. Either consciously or subconsciously, the marker on the mountain was always there.

Amy Baird Miner, a president of the BYU Student Association, told me on one occasion that the question most frequently asked by freshmen on this campus isn't "Where is the Cougareat?" or "Where do I cash a check?" Rather, it is "Who lights the Y?" I was informed that each year someone goes up there on the mountain in a helicopter and pushes the switch to light it up. It sounds easy enough, but it wasn't always done like that. Beginning in 1923, when the Y was lit for the first time, it was often lit when cotton bales or mattress stuffing dipped in pitch were set afire. It is currently lit by electricity with one thousand 25-watt bulbs. The Y, 380 feet tall and 130 feet wide, covers an area of 32,847 square feet and is said to be the largest school emblem in the world.

To understand what it means to light the Y today, we need to go back to some of the traditions of the past. In the early 1900s, freshmen students climbed to the letter each fall and removed brush from the area as part of their initiation activities. On Y Day in the spring, the students met early in the morning. After faculty members cleared the trail, the freshmen hauled water from a spring while sophomores carried up lime and salt and mixed it with the water in wooden troughs to make limestone. Then juniors and seniors poured the whitewash on the large letter. To keep up the workers' spirits, the school band played music all day.

A light on the mountain has much symbolism. Moses climbed Mount Sinai. There he saw God. There God spoke to him. There he received the Ten Commandments.

What does it mean to light the Y? It means that there are many mountains for each of us to climb. And when we find our Sinai and climb it, climb it to the top, there we will find God. He will speak to us, in our minds and in our hearts, by the spirit of revelation.

"For God, who commanded the light to shine out of darkness, hath shined in our hearts, to give the light of the knowledge of the glory of God in the face of Jesus Christ. But we have this treasure in earthen vessels, that the excellency of the power may be of God, and not of us." (2 Corinthians 4:6–7.)

Every individual has the right to and can have the Light of Christ in his life as an abiding influence, a personal guide. The Lord has promised, "I am the light of the world: he that followeth me shall not walk in darkness, but shall have the light of life." (John 8:12.) Truth, light, and spirit have a meaning linked to latter-day scripture: "The word of the Lord is truth, and whatsoever is truth is light, and whatsoever is light is Spirit, even the Spirit of Jesus Christ." (D&C 84:45.)

Some years ago, a faithful father gathered his children around on the occasion of family home evening. They were all in their places — mother, father, and each child, young and older. Together they sang a favorite song:

Teach me to walk in the light of his love;
Teach me to pray to my Father above;
Teach me to know of the things that are right;
Teach me, teach me to walk in the light.
— *Hymns*, no. 304

After a prayer inviting the Spirit of the Lord to be in that sacred setting, the father, looking into the eyes of each one present, said, "Tonight we're going to learn about the importance of walking in the light." Immediately the youngest child — too young, some may say, to be a teacher — spoke up with conviction: "Daddy, don't worry about me. I'll always walk in the light 'cause I'm scared of the dark." What a profound lesson taught in few words from a child. Do we know how to always walk in the light — and are we aware of the danger of the darkness?

The Savior taught the Nephites, "Behold, I am the law, and the light." (3 Nephi 15:9.) That, I believe, suggests a close and direct correlation between obedience to the law and the light available to us.

Lighting the Y on your mountain and mine means that we as individuals — every father, every mother, every son and daughter, brother and sister, friend, neighbor, and associate — bring light where there is darkness when we strive to live worthy of the blessings of the Lord, when we abide the law. Our obedience to law invades the darkness, dispels the darkness in the world, and thwarts the powers of the prince of darkness. Our duty is not only to walk in the light, but in so doing, to also dispel darkness. Light is the power of God. The scriptures state, "That which is of God is light; and he that receiveth light, and continueth in God, receiveth more light; and that light groweth brighter and brighter until the perfect day." (D&C 50:24.)

On one occasion President Harold B. Lee spoke concerning the lamp we each carry: "The Lord gives us, each one, a lamp to carry, but whether or not we shall have oil in our lamps depends solely upon each one of us. Whether or not we keep the commandments and supply the needed oil to light our way and to guide us on our way depends upon each of us individually. We cannot borrow from our Church membership. We cannot borrow from an illustrious ancestry. Whether or not we have oil in our lamps, I repeat, depends solely upon each one of us, it is determined by our faithfulness in keeping the commandments of the Living God. We must buy from the only source from which we can obtain this kind of oil referred to by the Master—from the fountain of eternal supply." (Conference Report, October 1951, p. 30.)

As Latter-day Saints who have taken upon us the name of Jesus Christ, we know of our responsibilities. We are called to "arise and shine forth, that [our] light may be a standard for the nations." (D&C 115:5.)

As we follow the light, share the light, become the light, and radiate the light, as a lighthouse in times of storm, we can help others navigate safely through troubled waters and guide them safely home.

The lighting of a nation begins in the heart and soul of each individual. I have visited many nations. I have looked into the faces and eyes of many young women. I have felt the strength and maturity of their spirits. I am aware of one young woman who, through the light within her, brought her father and sister back into activity in the Church. A twelve-year-old's testimony of faith was instrumental in touching the spirit of one who joined the Church in South America and later became a General Authority.

On one occasion I asked for a few noteworthy examples of students on BYU campus whose light has made a difference. I received impressive and heartwarming reports of many inspiring examples. One person wrote:

"There are literally hundreds of experiences of service rendered by the students here at BYU, but the ones I like the most are the little ones: the student helping the young mother with a stroller up the stairs from the bookstore to the Cougareat, a student pushing another in a wheelchair through the snow and ice, students opening doors for another who has books and packages in hand, students who clear off other students' car windows after the snowstorm has dumped inches of snow, a student helping other students learn mathematics, Chinese, and psychology, and students helping others to get their lives in order. All these acts of service are done on a daily basis practically without any thought at all."

Surely it is the little acts of service that help light the Y.

Someone has said, "Our agency is expressed in choosing or rejecting light." Every time we do right, we increase the light. Going contrary to the light within affects our power of concentration, our ability to learn, our access to light, and our ultimate success intellectually and spiritually. Every right choice, every good thought, every act of kindness, every commitment to obedience, every earnest prayer, every sacrifice in defense of truth, every ounce of self-discipline in response to the whisperings of the Spirit, every extra effort in diligent study and preparation, every honest act — these all add to the light. And when even one light gets dim or goes out as a result of wrong choices, the world is a little darker.

When we live with the Light of Christ in our lives, through our preparation and works of righteousness, we will contribute in a very real way to the dawning of a brighter day in a dark and troubled world. Today, with rapidly accelerated missionary work, thousands of people are accepting the gospel of Jesus Christ. He is the Light and the Life of the world. It is the Light of Jesus Christ that through us will burn brighter.

CHAPTER 7

The Night We
Bounced the Glo-Balls

What are we going to do?" shouted Bryce, tripping over
Spencer's sleeping bag. The narrow doorway did not
allow three enthusiastic boys with all their gear to enter
at once. "One thing for sure," Kent chuckled, remembering his
aunt's promise, "we're going to McDonald's for breakfast in the
morning, and we get to order anything we want. Egg McMuffin,
french fries, an apple turnover, and a Sprite for me." "Me too,"
came Spencer's quick response. And Bryce increased the order
to include scrambled eggs, sausage, and milk.

There was excitement in the air. It was the last Thursday
before school was to begin, and the warm summer sun, taking
its last peek of the day, was slipping behind the skyline and out
of sight beyond the lake. This day had been marked on the
calendar months before, at the end of the school year, which
had also marked the end of elementary school for these boys.
What had been referred to in the springtime as the long, hot
summer seemed now to have disappeared as quickly as cotton
candy melting in your mouth. Only a few days remained before
Kent, Bryce, and Spencer, in new blue jeans and shirts, would
assume an air of complete confidence, or so they hoped it would
appear, for their first day of junior high. There is security in
numbers, and loyal friends together can muster confidence even
while approaching the uncertain challenges of junior high. The
ninth graders always gave the impression of being big and brave,
the boys thought, and they must look no less the part, if possible.

But school was still a few days away, and any concerns could be postponed, at least for tonight.

A sleepover to be held at Kent's aunt's home had been a frequent topic of conversation between Kent and his friends during the hot summer months. Bryce's question, "What are we going to do?" was about to be answered.

It is impossible, I had thought the night before while cleaning up the house following a wedding reception at our home. *I cannot have those boys come tomorrow night. Maybe Saturday or, better still, next week.* With a good explanation, I was sure Kent would understand and the boys could come another time, since they seldom had conflicts in their schedules, and it would certainly be better for me.

There was no way of knowing when the promise was made in the springtime how impossible it would seem to me to crowd in one more event this week, even for Kent, and especially this day. Surely it wouldn't matter that much, my mind told me. *I'll call Kent early in the morning,* I thought, as I lay relaxed, the lights out and my eyes closed. Then I began to wonder. How did my Mom ever accomplish all she did?

In the darkness, my mind drifted back to years and years before. I remembered the day in the fall, just at harvest time, before school began. My mother was going to close our small country store in the late afternoon, a thing she had never done before. All summer long I had waited in anticipation of the promise she had made to take Colleen and me to Waterton Park to stay overnight. I had dreamed of the warm water in the swimming pool (quite different from swimming in the river), the playground, and the movie theater, none of which we had in our small town. Then the day we were to leave, the woman Mom had arranged to take care of the store called to say she had an emergency and could not come until the following day.

My disappointment was so intense that I felt a pain in the pit of my stomach. I thought I might throw up. I knew Mom wouldn't close the store now. I had heard her say a hundred times, "People expect us to be open until six o'clock, and we must be responsible and dependable." In a strange sort of way, I could feel that sick feeling all over my body as I stood at her side, too disappointed to even cry. And then I witnessed something I had never seen before. Mom took the money from the cash register, counted it out as she did at the close of every day, and placed the paper bills in a small metal box, leaving the coins in the till. As she carried the box to a room in the back, I followed her with hope awakening in my heart. She placed the tin box in the safe, turned the handle securely to lock it, and walked back to the front of the store. There she took the key from the little drawer beside the scale where we weighed things. She then took my hand and announced, "Like Dad says, 'a promise made is a debt unpaid.' We're going to go."

As she turned the key in the front door of our store, I knew as I had never known before how important I was. I was more important than all the customers who might come. I was more important than all the sales that might be made. My mother had always said I was special, but it was that afternoon so long ago that I understood.

"Yes," I told myself as I drifted off to sleep, "I'll call Kent in the morning to assure him everything is ready." There is anticipation that comes with waiting, but too much waiting can kill the spirit, the hope, the fun. I had promised the boys we'd do something fun to celebrate their readiness for junior high.

"Come in, come in. You're just in time," I greeted the boys at the door the next evening. "Just drop your things where they are." They waited for further instructions. "Get in my car," I directed. "We're heading for the planetarium."

"The planetarium!" they exclaimed. "Wow!" said Kent, giving his approval for the plan.

"The show for tonight is 'Cosmic Catastrophes,'" I explained, beginning to feel some excitement myself for this promise I had determined to keep.

The boys climbed in the back seat of my car, and I chauffeured them to town, listening to their chatter all the way. "It will be a blast," Kent told his friends. Having visited the planetarium before, he assumed a leadership position for this important event. He explained how, with a small keyboard in front of each seat, you could make a difference in what would appear on the dome-shaped ceiling that looks like the night sky. As the lights went down and the show began, I observed that the boys responded to the questions on the screen with great enthusiasm, as if they were in effect controlling some aspect of the universe and maybe even the galaxies. Observing their excitement was even more enjoyable for me than watching the show—until I dozed off to sleep.

When the show was over and the lights came up, I had had a little rest. There were several hours left before the day would be over for these eager young boys, and I was ready.

Immediately they became interested in the items available for purchase in the lobby of the planetarium. As they examined several items with longing, I invited them to each select one item as a reminder of our evening together and I would buy it for them. It takes a long time to choose when so many things appear of equal interest. After vacillating back and forth and consulting with each other, all three boys agreed on the same purchase. They each selected a Glo-ball—a bright pink ball about the size of a large button on their father's overcoat.

While I paid for the purchase, the boys ran ahead, down the stairs, out onto the sidewalk, bouncing their Glo-balls all the way. The sky was dark now except for the stars, which appeared very much like those in the simulated sky in the cosmic show. But the street lights provided ample light for bouncing and chasing balls. Would this be an experience they would remember? I wondered, as I watched them run back and forth, in and out, bumping into each other, laughing, and competing in their attempts to bounce their balls higher and higher.

"Mine goes the highest," was Spencer's claim. "Yeah, but mine goes farther," Bryce called out as he chased his out-of-control Glo-ball down the steps and past the fountain.

After some time, I suggested to the boys that we stroll over to Temple Square. They looked at each other to get a consensus and halfheartedly agreed.

As they approached the large iron gates on the south side of Temple Square, bouncing the Glo-balls all the way, the boys came to an abrupt stop. On the street in front of the gates were a police car, two policemen, and three young men dressed in old and tattered black clothing. Walking a little closer, we observed that one of the young men was wearing handcuffs and the other two were being pushed into the car. The boys pocketed their Glo-balls in their palms and stood and watched silently. A few minutes later the car drove away with the young men and the police officers.

Spencer finally broke the silence. "Those guys must really have messed up," he said. Bryce and Kent responded in unison, "Yeah."

Just inside the gate an elderly gentleman in a dark suit, white shirt, and tie greeted the boys with such warmth and kindness that it was as though he had been expecting them. "Come in, boys. Please come in," he said, extending both arms. It was quiet on the grounds. Only a few visitors could be seen strolling through the gardens. Indirect lighting placed at regular intervals along the garden paths cast a glow over the entire block.

"I wonder where those guys will sleep tonight," Kent said. "In jail," was Spencer's quick reply. "Do you think their parents know where they are?" asked Bryce. Their concern for the three young men was evident.

The spectacular array of flowers in a profusion of fall colors captured my full attention. For the boys, those Glo-balls held tightly in their hands demanded release. It was as though they could be contained no longer. All three balls escaped at once, and the boys were soon laughing and enjoying their activity as before. I wondered about the propriety of their conduct in this setting and glanced over at the gentleman at the gate. Judging from his smile, I regretted that I had not purchased a Glo-ball for him. As he watched those energetic young boys, I sensed he might have liked to join them, or maybe he was just thinking back on a time when he was a boy, perhaps a time when someone took him and his friends to play ball.

In a short time the fun of bouncing the Glo-balls took on an added challenge. Kent, in his usual inquisitive way, made a quick discovery. "Look, you guys," he said, holding his ball next to one of the lights along the path, "it really does glow." Bryce immediately tested his. "Mine does too," he announced. And so it did, as did each of the balls when held next to one of the lights along the path.

The boys' concern was no longer how high the balls would go, but how long could they bounce a ball after holding it next to the source of light before it would begin to lose its light. Spencer launched the experiment. As the glow from his ball diminished, the boys began trying to locate the next closest source of light. The competition between them was no longer apparent. Bryce was not trying to outdo Spencer; Kent no longer showed any concern that Bryce's ball went higher than his; and Spencer was totally consumed with the light he was trying to collect and keep for his own ball. The distance between each source of light and how quickly each boy could run from one to the next became the obvious challenge.

I watched Kent on his knees, rolling the little Glo-ball between his stubby fingers, holding it close to the source of light along the path. He then cupped the ball tightly between his hands, jumped to his feet, and ran quickly to the next closest light. Opening his hands, he shouted triumphantly, "I did it! I did it!" Kent explained, holding up his ball with obvious delight, "I can go so fast from one light to the next that this ball stays bright. If you can go fast enough, it can always glow." Bryce and Spencer dropped to their knees next to him to verify his claim. Bryce made the same discovery and added, "But you gotta have lights and they gotta be close." Spencer agreed. "If they turned off the lights, it wouldn't work."

The boys continued testing their theory and became convinced. "There's got to be a source of light. You can't store it up. You have to go after it, and you'd better run fast."

The boys had made a great discovery, and so had I. *Yes,* I thought, *if you boys have learned this lesson, you're ready for junior high and much, much more.*

I was surprised when I looked at my watch to see how late it was. *We should be leaving for home,* I thought, but junior high was only a few days away, and there would be structured lessons outlined on the pages of the various textbooks. Lessons would be followed by the pressure of examinations to determine the level of understanding and supposedly measure one's learning ability. Tonight there were lessons but no formal tests—lessons to learn and hopefully remember.

"Boys," I said, "would you tuck your Glo-balls in your pocket and come with me?" We did not head toward the gate, as they supposed. Instead we found a bench between the visitors' center and the Salt Lake Temple with its softly lighted spires reaching heavenward, illuminating the night sky. Kent, assuming some responsibility for the interest of his friends, asked, "What are we going to do now?"

I sat on the bench and motioned to the boys. They joined me, Bryce on one side, Kent and Spencer on the other. "We're going to talk," I said. I looked toward the spires of the temple and they did the same. There was silence. In a moment Kent asked, "About what?"

"About Glo-balls," I said. "Real Glo-balls."

I pondered the possibility, the potential, the gifts and talents, eagerness and youthfulness, of these young boys and continued, "Kent, Spencer, and Bryce, you are the real Glo-balls. You have the light within. You can shine in darkness. You can light up the world. You can help dispel the darkness. You can make a difference." I paused, then added, "If you want to."

Bryce's response was quick. "How?" he asked. I disregarded his question for a moment, hoping to provide a more complete answer a little later. Instead I commented, "I've been thinking about those boys who were taken away in the police car. I wonder what will happen to them."

"They'll go to jail," was a quick response. "They're bad."

I nodded in agreement. "I wonder when they became bad." I waited and then asked my next question: "Were they born bad?" The boys shook their heads. Kent insisted, "You're not born bad."

"Then when did it happen, and where were their friends who might have helped them? Do you think those young men are saying their prayers?" All three boys shook their heads. "Or reading their scriptures?" Again they shook their heads. "Or going to church? Or keeping the commandments?"

A verbal response was given this time. "No, they're not."

"Do you think they're serving others or care much about others?"

Again there was an audible response. "I don't think so," Kent said. "Me either," echoed Bryce.

We sat in silence for a few moments. Each boy was quiet with his own thoughts, maybe reflecting on his feelings and habits concerning prayer, scripture study, obedience, and service. Coming back to the point of the lesson, I looked first at Bryce on my left and then Kent and Spencer on my right. "Boys," I said, with all the conviction I could convey in my voice, "you are the real Glo-balls—and whether you just bounce along in the dark trying to get higher and higher than the next or whether you decide to run from one source of light to the next and always be bright is something you might want to think about."

As if it were a moment for a public declaration of personal commitment, the boys stood up. Spencer didn't need time to think. "We're not gonna be in the dark," he said. "We'll glow in the dark," came Kent's response.

"How?" I asked.

The answer was obvious. Bryce put it into words. "Stay near the light," he said.

"Boys," I said, "Jesus has taught us about light. In the Sermon on the Mount he tells us, 'Ye are the light of the world. . . . Let your light so shine before men, that they may see your good works, and glorify your Father which is in heaven.' It's a spiritual light," I explained, "a light within you that comes from your Father in heaven. You can keep your light bright always."

The boys sat on the little bench again, and they were quiet for a few moments. Kent finally broke the silence. "But what about those guys the police took?" he asked.

I remembered a scripture about light and shared it with the boys. "Jesus said, 'I am the light of the world: he that followeth me shall not walk in darkness, but shall have the light of life.' " (John 8:12.) I waited, wondering if this was a lesson better taught at another time. Spencer spoke up. "How does the light get in us?"

As I searched for some way to help them understand and remember, a thought came into my mind. I asked them what must have seemed to be a totally unrelated question. "What does it mean when someone says, 'Give 'em five' and then raises his hand high in the air to be slapped by a friend's hand?" The boys jumped from the bench and slapped each other's hands, while all three attempted to explain at once. "It means everything's good. It means we won the game. It means we're great."

"Okay, boys," I went on, "together we're going to discover how your fingers and your thumb can remind you of how to get the light inside, the spiritual light, so you won't ever forget. Okay?"

"Okay," they responded, wide-eyed and curious.

Holding the thumb on my left hand straight up, I asked the boys to do the same. They did. "When you kneel down," I said, "what does it remind you of?"

"To say your prayers," was Kent's response.

I then bent my thumb and asked, "Don't you think this looks like a praying thumb?" The boys bent their own thumbs to check. "When you bend your thumb, it will remind you of the importance of prayer," I explained. "Prayer is an important source of spiritual light." The boys practiced bending their thumbs, first on the left hand and then the right.

Next I extended my finger and asked, "What do we call this finger?"

"The pointer finger," was Spencer's response. All three boys extended their pointer fingers and waited for an explanation.

I wanted them to provide the explanation, so I introduced the next question. "What do we have that points the way, that gives us direction, that tells us what to do, like reading instructions, like a map?"

This time Spencer responded first. "The scriptures. They point the way."

I agreed, explaining that I like to think of my scriptures as letters from home, messages from our Father in heaven to guide us day by day. And then I emphasized the fact that our scriptures are another important source of light.

With my hand wide open and held straight up, I suggested that our tallest finger could be a reminder of the tallest spire on the temple, like the one located just in front of us. "What can the temple finger remind you of?" was my next question as the boys held their hands straight up and examined their tallest finger. "What must you do if you want the blessings of the temple?" I asked.

Kent responded quickly and without any hesitation. "You keep the commandments," he said.

"Another source of light," I added.

As I raised the fourth finger on my left hand, the answer came before I asked. "That's the ring finger, the marriage finger," Spencer said.

"And what does marriage remind you of?"

The idea of his finger reminding him of marriage caused Kent to respond in a joking tone. "Love," he said.

"And service," I added. "That's another source of light."

Inviting a quick review, I raised my thumb once again and bent it. Without any coaching, the boys did the same and, in unison, raising first their thumbs and then each finger in turn, repeated, "Prayer, scripture study, keep the commandments, and love and service."

One finger was left, and they waited for an explanation.

"Do you remember when you were very young and your mom taught you about where the little pig went?" I asked.

The answer came at once. "All the way home." They giggled as they wiggled their little fingers.

With my hand held out and my fingers spread wide, I asked the boys the question Bryce had asked: "How can you get the light inside?"

Without coaching, the boys, holding their hands high as in a "high-five," repeated in unison: "Prayer, scripture study, keeping the commandments, love and service, and all the way home."

I rehearsed for them once again the lesson, adding the importance of daily prayer, daily scripture study, daily keeping the commandments, and daily giving love and service. "These are all sources of light, boys, that will help you get the light inside, and one day they take you all the way home, safely, to your Father in heaven."

As I stood up, the boys jumped to their feet, spontaneously giving each other a "high-five," and including me as we slapped our hands together promising to remember. Then we returned to the car and headed for home.

It was two o'clock before the boys finished their treats, rolled out their sleeping bags, silenced their talking, and finally drifted off to sleep. Morning came early, and junior high was one day closer. Kent's first comment was a reminder of my promise to take them to McDonald's for breakfast. There was time to keep my promise, time to build memories, time to learn lessons, time to show Kent and his friends they are important, and time for breakfast.

The boys climbed into the car, a little quieter than the night before, perhaps from lack of sleep. We drove north to McDonald's. I pulled into the parking lot and suddenly, as if a fire alarm had sounded, they were wide awake. "Come on, you guys," Kent called out, leading the way. Inside the restaurant, he placed his order without hesitation: "One Egg McMuffin, french fries, an apple turnover, and a Sprite." And then he added, "A small order of Chicken McNuggets." He confidently reminded Spencer and Bryce they could order anything they wanted. Hash browns, hot cakes, scrambled eggs, and sausage, along with milk and hot chocolate, were included in their combined menu.

Following breakfast, with only a few french fries left on one of the plates and their stomachs full, Kent raised his hand high in the air. Bryce and Spencer responded, slapping his hand, then each other's. They stood in the corner by the table at McDonald's and, beginning with the kneeling thumb and followed by each finger, reviewed in unison their lesson of the night before: "Prayer, scripture study, keep the commandments, love and service." Then they slapped their hands together again in a "high-five," confirming the conviction that it would take them "all the way home."

The boys are now halfway through junior high, and many lessons have been learned, with many more left to master. But often when I see them, they volunteer a "high-five" and slap my hand in remembrance of the night we bounced Glo-balls. And then I remember the day my mom kept her promise and took me and my friend to Waterton Park.

One day when Kent, Bryce, and Spencer are serving as missionaries, maybe in some faraway land, they will share their light from within. They will stand as special witnesses for Jesus Christ. They will teach others how to seek the light, find the light, and follow the light. They will teach them that the light of Christ is within. Maybe when they place their hands on someone's head to pronounce a blessing, they will look at their fingers and remember the source of light and how you get the light inside. And they will remember the night they bounced the Glo-balls on Temple Square.

CHAPTER 8

Will We
Return Home Safely?

Not long ago I sat in the large assembly room at the Missionary Training Center surrounded by newly arriving missionaries and anxious parents and other family members. As the final instructions were being given to the missionaries, I became aware of the man sitting next to me. His hands indicated that he was probably a laborer; his clothing was well worn. His head was bowed, perhaps to hide what may have been a tear as he took his handkerchief from his pocket. Then I glanced at the young man sitting next to him, apparently his missionary son. He was looking straight ahead, with a sober expression on his face, and appeared to be ignoring his father. I wondered if perhaps he was embarrassed by his father's appearance, or maybe they didn't have a good relationship.

At soon as the instructions were completed and the meeting was dismissed, it was as though the young man could not control his emotions one moment longer. It didn't matter that he was surrounded by people. It didn't matter that he was nineteen years old. It didn't matter that others might be watching. Try as he might, he could no longer control his emotions. While his tears flowed freely, he wrapped his arms around his father like parentheses, closed his eyes, and held him very close. The older man, also with tears in his eyes, returned his son's embrace. As I watched this tender scene, I wondered about the sacrifice that was being made and if the young man was going on his mission because his father was sending him. Would there be difficult times when he would like to turn back? Would people accept him and his message? Would he return home safely? Would it be worth it?

Those who have raised a missionary son or daughter from the time that a Band-Aid bandage and a kiss could cure all ills, until that little boy or girl, suddenly older, is ready to be sent forth as a representative of the Lord Jesus Christ, can relate to these feelings. Even a close relative is not too far removed to sense a yearning, to be assured that the missionary will be cared for and will return home safely at the appointed time.

But can any of us, in any possible way, begin to comprehend even in the smallest part what it meant for God the Father to send his Son on his mission to earth, knowing what must come to pass if he were to finish the work he volunteered to do? And how could the Son, even the Son of God, say to the Father, "Thy will be done," knowing what would be required?

May I share with you an account given by Elder Melvin J. Ballard many years ago relating to this singular event in all of history.

> What father and mother could stand by and listen to the cry of their children in distress . . . and not render assistance? I have heard of mothers throwing themselves into raging streams when they could not swim a stroke to save their drowning children, [of fathers] rushing into burning buildings to rescue those whom they loved. We cannot stand by and listen to those cries without it touching our hearts. . . .
>
> [God] had the power to save and He loved His Son, and He could have saved Him. He might have rescued Him from the insult of the crowds. He might have rescued Him when the crown of thorns was placed upon His head. He might have rescued Him when the Son, hanging between two thieves, was mocked with, "Save thyself, and come down from the cross. He saved others; himself he cannot save." He listened to all this. He saw that Son condemned; He saw Him drag the cross through the streets of Jerusalem and faint under its load. He saw the Son finally upon Calvary; He saw His body stretched out upon the wooden cross; He saw the cruel nails driven

through hands and feet, and the blows that broke the skin, tore the flesh, and let out the life's blood of His [Only Begotten] Son. . . .

[God] looked on [all that] with great grief and agony over His Beloved [Son], until there seems to have come a moment when even our Saviour cried out in despair: "My God, my God, why hast thou forsaken me?"

In that hour I think I can see our dear Father behind the veil looking upon these dying struggles, . . . His great heart almost breaking for the love that He had for His Son. Oh, in that moment when He might have saved His Son, I thank Him and praise Him that He did not fail us. . . . I rejoice that He did not interfere, and that His love for us made it possible for Him to endure to look upon the sufferings of His [Only Begotten] and give Him finally to us, our Saviour and our Redeemer. Without Him, without His sacrifice, we would have remained, and we would never have come glorified into His presence. . . . This is what it cost, in part, for our Father in heaven to give the gift of His Son, unto men . . . his greatest gift unto us. (*Melvin J. Ballard, Crusader for Righteousness*, Salt Lake City: Bookcraft, 1966, pp. 136–38.)

Some years ago my husband and I, with a small group of friends, stood silently in the Garden of Gethsemane in the Holy City, each pondering our own thoughts and feelings. We walked where Jesus had walked and felt his presence there. The old, gnarled olive trees were bent and reaching toward the ground, the same trees, I suppose, that were there the very night the Savior of the world went into the Garden of Gethsemane and willingly took upon himself the sins of the world. His suffering was beyond human power to endure. He was the Son of God, and yet he willingly "suffered the pain of all men, that all men might repent and come unto him." (D&C 18:11.)

In the quiet moments in the Garden of Gethsemane, I wondered how in this world could we ever express gratitude for the Savior and his sacrifice for us. The thought came: We express our gratitude by the choices and decisions we make each day of our lives. The Lord said, "If ye love me, keep my commandments." (John 14:15.)

In the premortal existence, the Savior had determined his course and, even knowing what would be required, was willing to pay the price for our sins and our souls. He said in the council, "Father, thy will be done, and the glory be thine forever." (Moses 4:2.) He came to earth—the Son of God, our Savior, our Redeemer, our Brother—to do the will of the Father.

At the close of his earthly ministry, he was taken to the place called Calvary, and there he was crucified. The terrifying events of that Friday hung heavily over the land that day and the next, and then a faint streak of dawn broke through the darkness of the first great Easter morning. On Sunday morning, while it was still dark, an angel of the Lord descended from the heavens and rolled back the massive stone, thus opening the tomb. The tomb now stood open—and empty.

In the early dawn, Mary Magdalene, whose love and devotion had caused her to linger at the cross, now came to the tomb. Burdened with grief, she stooped again to look into the empty tomb. There she beheld two angels in white, one sitting at the head and one at the foot where the body of Jesus had lain. One of the angels spoke to her in gentle tones and said, "Woman, why weepest thou?" Her troubled soul responded to the haunting thought: "They have taken away my Lord, and I know not where they have laid him." With her whole heart consumed by the anxiety of the moment, Mary did not recognize the person standing close by. That person asked her with compassion, "Woman, why weepest thou? whom seekest thou?" Thinking him the gardener, she pleaded, "Sir, if thou have borne him hence, tell me where thou hast laid him, and I will take him away." She desired even yet to care for her Lord.

In the quiet of that garden setting, in the springtime of the year and the freshness of a new day, he spoke her name: "Mary." One word turned her grief to joy. She recognized the tone of his voice. She recognized him. Uttering the title "Rabboni," which is to say, "Master," she reached out to him. Jesus gently restrained her, explaining, "Touch me not; for I am not yet ascended to my Father: but go to my brethren, and say unto them, I ascend unto my Father, and your Father; and to my God, and your God." (John 20:13–17.)

Until now no mortal person had ever beheld a resurrected being. Mary Magdalene was the first to witness this glorious event. The joy in her heart carried her away in great haste, eager to share the remarkable news with the others that there was no need for mourning and weeping. She delivered her message, the most significant of all recorded history: "He is risen." (Mark 16:6.)

Jesus was alive! He was resurrected from the dead! She had seen him! Though her joy was great, however, it could not be shared, for we read, "They . . . believed not." (Mark 16:11.) This event was so extraordinary that even the apostles, who had been carefully taught, could not yet grasp the reality of it. Millions of individuals had lived and died during the course of earth's history to that day, "but until that first Easter morning not one had risen from the grave." (See Marion G. Romney, "The Resurrection of Jesus," *Ensign*, May 1982, p. 6.)

When time stands still and the veil seems very thin, questions flood into our minds. "He did all of that for me, though he didn't have to? But he did! Whatever he asks of us, is it too much? Maybe it is not enough. Surely it is not enough." In the silence of our hearts, we feel a burning conviction, a personal testimony that he did that for us. And then the awesome thought, "What if, just what if, he paid that awesome price for me, to redeem me, to save me, to be my personal Savior, and that price was paid in vain in my behalf because in my daily life I choose not to do my part?"

What is our part? How do we express our gratitude? How do we always remember and never forget? It is the sacrament, the holy priesthood ordinance, that helps remind us of the Savior's atonement and our sacred covenants. It is a precious and sacred reminder, not just on Sunday, but on Monday, Tuesday, and Wednesday, spring, summer, and fall, when we are on the mountain peaks of our lives but maybe even more so in the valleys. It is often in the valleys with our afflictions that we are truly humbled and better prepared to remember the gift of eternal life for which he paid the price — those times when we feel least worthy, least comfortable about carrying his holy name, and have a keener sense of our imperfections, those moments when the flesh is weak and our spirits suffer disappointment for our errors and our sins. We might feel a sense of withdrawal, a pulling away, a feeling of needing to set aside for a time at least that divine relationship with the Savior until we are more worthy. But at that very moment, even in our unworthiness, the offer is again given to us to accept the great gift of the Atonement — even before we change. When we feel the need to pull away, let us reach out to him. Instead of feeling the need to resist, let us submit to his will. Let us bend our will as well as our knees in humble supplication.

May I share with you the words of Elder David B. Haight concerning the sacrament:

> Jesus gave Himself — His body and His blood — as a ransom for our sins. He sacrificed His life so that we might live again. We eat in remembrance of His body. We remember the Passover, the Last Supper, Gethsemane, Calvary, and the Resurrection. His blood represents a new testament — a new covenant with Israel. We drink in remembrance of His suffering — a suffering so excruciating that He said it "caused myself, even God, the greatest of all, to tremble because of pain, and to bleed at every pore, and to suffer both body and spirit — and would that I might not drink the bitter cup, and shrink — Nevertheless, glory be to the Father, and I partook and finished my preparations unto the children of men" (D&C 19:18–19). ("Remembering the Savior's Atonement," *Ensign,* April 1988, p. 9.)

We are to partake of the sacrament worthily. And what constitutes worthiness? I believe it requires that we take a little inventory of ourselves, a personal interview, on a daily basis. Are our hearts pure? Do we hear the whisperings of the Holy Ghost? Do we listen to our conscience?

C. S. Lewis has written, "The more you obey your conscience, the more your conscience will demand of you. And your natural self, which is thus being starved and hampered and worried at every turn, will get angrier and angrier." According to Lewis, it is as though Jesus were saying to each of us: "Give me All. I don't want so much of your time and so much of your money and so much of your work: I want You. I have not come to torment your natural self, but to kill it. . . . Hand over the whole natural self. . . . I will give you a new self instead. In fact, I will give you Myself: my own will shall become yours." (*Mere Christianity*, New York: Macmillan, 1960, p. 167.)

When we want what Jesus wants, we will get all that we want and much, much more. We will become joint-heirs with him and receive all of the blessings the Father has promised. If these eternal truths seem almost beyond comprehension and faith falters, be not discouraged. Alma teaches us:

"Faith is not to have a perfect knowledge of things; therefore if ye have faith ye hope for things which are not seen, which are true.

"And now, behold, I say unto you, and I would that ye should remember, that God is merciful unto all who believe on his name; therefore he desireth, in the first place, that ye should believe, yea, even on his word. . . .

"But behold, if ye will awake and arouse your faculties, even to an experiment upon my words, and exercise a particle of faith, yea, even if ye can no more than desire to believe, let this desire work in you, even until ye believe in a manner that ye can give place for a portion of my words.

"Now, we will compare the word unto a seed. Now, if ye give place, that a seed may be planted in your heart, behold, if it be a true seed, or a good seed, if ye do not cast it out by your unbelief, that ye will resist the Spirit of the Lord, behold, it will begin to swell within your breasts." (Alma 32:21–22; 27–28.)

Wherever we find ourselves at this time in our life's experiences, may God bless us with unwavering faith to know that the mission of the Savior—his death, followed by his resurrection on that first Easter morning—is as efficacious today as it was two thousand years ago. With our limited perspective, and with the sobering reality of our imperfections and that turbulence in our hearts caused by that distance between where we are and where we want to be, let us remember that it is by the grace of God that we are made whole.

There is no doubt in my mind that the father I saw at the Missionary Training Center will count the days, the weeks, and the months until his son returns home. And in that great reunion, the father will humbly say, "This is my boy, my son, in whom I am well pleased."

May we too hear in our minds the words of the Savior speaking to each of us: "If ye will come unto me ye shall have eternal life. Behold, mine arm of mercy is extended towards you, and whosoever will come, him will I receive; and blessed are those who come unto me. . . .

"Behold, I have come unto the world to bring redemption unto the world, to save the world from sin. Therefore, whoso repenteth and cometh unto me as a little child, him will I receive, for of such is the kingdom of God. Behold, for such I have laid down my life, and have taken it up again; therefore repent, and come unto me ye ends of the earth, and be saved." (3 Nephi 9:14, 21–22.)

One day at the close of our earthly mission, because of our Lord and Savior, Jesus Christ, our Redeemer, we too will return home to our Father. Let us live with the anticipation of that glorious day. I believe we will come running, and with outstretched arms our Father will greet us, and we will respond, "Oh, my Father, I am home again." Then if we have done our part, by his grace we will receive our inheritance as his sons and daughters, his heirs, and joint-heirs with our Elder Brother, Jesus Christ.

CHAPTER 9

Doubt Not, Fear Not

The other day a friend of mine approaching her fortieth birthday asked me in all seriousness, "How did you handle the middle-age crisis?" I told her, "I don't. I haven't reached it yet." Somewhat surprised and curious, she asked, "Well, how old are you?" I told her this was my big year, sixty. She smiled and said, "Oh, you've reached it all right. You just don't remember."

Maybe that is a case of forgetfulness or denial or being out of touch with reality. It has been said that with each passing year one is found dealing more and more frequently with the hereafter. You go from one room to the next and wonder, "Now what was it I came here after?"

In all seriousness I believe it is, in fact, an awareness of the hereafter that provides the spiritual dimension for our lives today. As we learn to view our experiences in this life with the perspective of eternity, we tend to draw away from the things of the world that pull us apart and to feel closer to the things of the Spirit that keep us whole. When the reality of eternity presses upon our minds and we are guided by the Spirit, we begin to view life differently. The Apostle Paul expressed this thought: "We look not at the things which are seen, but at the things which are not seen: for the things which are seen are temporal; but the things which are not seen are eternal." (2 Corinthians 4:18.)

He also reminds us: "For they that are after the flesh do

mind the things of the flesh; but they that are after the Spirit the things of the Spirit. For to be carnally minded is death; but to be spiritually minded is life and peace." (Romans 8:5–6.)

Looking back over the years, I realize that one's spiritual dimension comes as a gradual process. We don't ordinarily remember the specific time we learned to read or to walk, nor do we remember the day we gained our faith, although we may well remember those occasions when it has been tried and tested. Elder Neal A. Maxwell reminded us that "adversity can increase faith." ("Lest Ye Be Wearied and Faint in Your Minds," *Ensign*, May 1991, p. 88.) Moroni taught us about the need for our faith to be tried: "Wherefore, dispute not because ye see not, for ye receive no witness until after the trial of your faith." (Ether 12:6.) President Brigham Young addressed our need for challenges when he said, "The men and women who desire to obtain seats in the celestial kingdom will find that they must battle every day." (*Discourses of Brigham Young,* Salt Lake City: Deseret Book, 1954, p. 392.)

From the pivotal point where I now stand looking back threescore years and forward to eternity, I would like to share a brief brushstroke from my own experience that may be a pattern for others as we all strive to nourish the seed and partake of the fruits of faith.

At an early age, I had the faith of a little child. I believed anything was possible. I knew what I wanted and when I wanted it. Perhaps you are familiar with the thought, "Please, Lord, teach me patience, right now."

In time, with more experience, I became more patient and willing to wait with faith in a loving Father, hoping that it wouldn't be too long before my prayers were answered—"a few weeks or even months maybe, but please, Father, not years." I learned that often it is during the waiting, when we are in the valleys and not on the mountain peaks, that the greatest progress is made. Eventually we no longer need to have things our way. Experience teaches us that our Heavenly Father knows what is best and that all we need or want to know is his will. We learn to bend our will as well as our knees, and to yield our hearts with only one desire in mind: "What, Father, would you have me do? I want to know your will and I want to carry it out. Please, will you reveal it to me?"

Is there any one who has not had occasion to cry out at some time and plead with a burning desire to reach and stretch far enough to connect with God? He tells us, "Draw near unto me and I will draw near unto you." (D&C 88:63.) After extended periods of fasting and prayer, have we not asked, "But, Father, what more can I do? What should I understand about working by faith?"

Then one day in our progress we gain a new and wonderful dimension. We learn to hang on and we learn to let go. We learn to differentiate between the things we must hold to tenaciously and those we must let go of if our faith is to grow. This is a mighty step in our spiritual development. We no longer need to have things our way, not now, not ever. We don't need all of the answers and we don't need additional promises. We begin to understand more fully the scripture, "Trust in the Lord with all thine heart; and lean not unto thine own understanding. In all thy ways acknowledge him, and he shall direct thy paths." (Proverbs 3:5–6.)

Our faith will be tried and tested with each generation, and how we respond will have a tremendous impact on future generations. We catch this message in a familiar hymn: "Faith of our fathers, holy faith, / We will be true to thee till death!" (*Hymns*, no. 84.)

An abiding faith in the Lord Jesus Christ—his birth, his life, his resurrection, and the atonement—gives direction and brings light where there is darkness, hope where there is despair, and peace in place of torment. At times when the challenges of this life press down upon me, I think of my faithful, noble mother, of her strength and indomitable spirit. I think of my beloved grandmother who left England and my great-grandmother who stayed behind, and I feel a connection, a heritage of faith.

Many other great women helped nourish the seeds of faith

in my tender years. I think of dear old Sister Bertha Buck, who often stood by her white picket fence covered with gooseberry bushes when I was on my way to school each day and raised her hand and called, "God bless you, my child." And because she asked God to bless me, I knew he would. I think of Sister Myrtle Dudley, my Primary teacher, who wore the same maroon dress to Primary every week. I remember her tired eyes, her thin gray hair, and her big smile. I thought she was beautiful. She taught me songs of faith. And Martha Shipley, who never married and had no posterity. She came to our home day after day to help my mother when I was young, and while there she taught me by her example about service and sacrifice and faith. I sense a powerful and very real heritage of faith transmitted by these good women from one generation to the next.

Paul, speaking to Timothy, tells his young friend to look to his mother and his grandmother in consideration of his own faith: "When I call to remembrance the unfeigned faith that is in thee, which dwelt first in thy grandmother Lois, and thy mother Eunice; and I am persuaded that in thee also. Wherefore I put thee in remembrance that thou stir up the gift of God, which is in thee by the putting on of my hands. For God hath not given us the spirit of fear; but of power, and of love, and of a sound mind." (2 Timothy 1:5–7.)

Two thousand young men known as the stripling warriors knew, because of the teachings of their mothers, that God would deliver them. "We do not doubt our mothers knew it," they said. (See Alma 56:47–48.) Is it any wonder that President Gordon B. Hinckley has said, "When a girl is saved, a generation is saved"? ("Youth Is the Season," *New Era*, September 1988, p. 47.)

Some good women may be the first in their line to establish a strong heritage of faith. Others may inherit faith from past generations. In either case, the spiritual dimensions of a woman's faith weave themselves through the tapestry of eternity from one generation to the next.

President Spencer W. Kimball, speaking to the women of

the Church, said, "To be a righteous woman is a glorious thing in any age. To be a righteous woman during the winding-up scene on this earth, before the second coming of our Savior, is an especially noble calling. The righteous woman's strength and influence today can be tenfold what it might be in more tranquil times." ("Privileges and Responsibilities of Sisters," *Ensign*, November 1978, p. 103.)

In the rededicatory prayer of the St. George Temple in November 1975, President Kimball prayed: "We again ask thy blessing on the women in all the land that they may accomplish the measure of their creation as daughters of God, thy offspring. Let the blessings of Sarah, Hulda, Hannah, Anna, and Mary the mother of the Son of God, bless these women to fulfill their duties as did Mary, our beloved mother of Thy Son, and let the power and satisfactions of the prophetesses and all holy women rest upon these mothers as they have moved forward to fulfill their destinies."

And now, looking back over the years with a much different perspective, I am glad God allows us to struggle, to cry, and to feel pain, else how could we comfort others in their tribulation?

I am glad we know about hurt and healing, else how would we know the Healer, the Great Physician, who invites us to come unto him and be healed?

I am glad we know about fear and faith, else how would we recognize the light of faith after the dark night of fear?

I am glad we know about offenses and forgiveness, else how could we ever begin to appreciate the Atonement?

I am glad we know about discouragement and encouragement, else how could we reach out and take another's hand in empathy, understanding, and love?

I am grateful to know about the grace of God and his infinite love for each of us.

It is with faith in God's eternal plan that our spiritual dimension is expanded, enlarged, magnified. He is our Father; we are indeed his children.

Oh, if only it could be said of every woman what Joseph F.

Smith said of Eliza R. Snow: "She walked not in the borrowed light of others but faced the morning unafraid and invincible."

My niece Shelly Larsen, a young woman of faith who carried the message of the gospel of Jesus Christ to the people in New Zealand, wrote the following in a letter home: "I love the gospel and know it is true because the Spirit has let me know by touching my heart. The Spirit of the Lord enriches my life daily, and I am so excited to share this happiness with my brothers and sisters in New Zealand. I love my Savior, and I am so amazed and grateful for the love He has for me. I am thankful for His Atonement and for the blessings His sacrifice brings into my life. I am grateful for the power of prayer and that I can talk to my Father in Heaven, and I know He hears and answers my prayers. The power of prayer and the Holy Ghost, which powers I am so humble and grateful to be able to receive, bless my life every day. I know that Joseph Smith is a prophet of God and that he actually saw God the Father and Jesus Christ. I love the Book of Mormon and love the spirit it brings into my life."

I too bear testimony of the things that Shelly knows to be true. These are the fruits of faith to be passed on to generations yet to come. My faith has not moved mountains. My faith has not parted the Red Sea. My faith has not brought desired answers to all my prayers, although I have prayed fervently and tried to live faithfully. But of this I bear testimony: I have witnessed many, many miracles, especially during the years I have worked with and for the young women of the Church.

Through my faith and prayers and fasting, mingled with that of my sisters and other family members, I have witnessed a miracle in the life of a loved one who was lost and spiritually dead. After many years, by the grace of God this loved one lives again. God bless us to walk by faith, and in so doing, to leave a legacy of faith, a rich heritage of faith for generations of young women and young men yet to come. Remember the words of our Savior, "Look unto me in every thought; doubt not, fear not." (D&C 6:36.)

TRAVELING
TOGETHER

CHAPTER 10

Take Hold of Hands
and Hang On Tight

The Salt Lake City airport was unusually crowded that morning. A mass of humanity moving along the concourse formed an irregular pattern of coming and going. The "crossroads of the West" was evident as planes circled overhead waiting for the signal indicating each pilot's turn to deposit passengers, some for connecting flights and others returning home to the valley of the Great Salt Lake.

Inside the airport, small clusters of people gathered, forming a microcosm in a world all their own. Emotions were high, and tears filled the eyes of some. A father in a warm jacket and well-worn trousers gave his son a last embrace as the young man, in white shirt and new dark suit, tried to hold back his tears. While some people were hanging on to the minutes ticking away too fast, hoping to prolong the time before departure as long as possible, others impatiently waited for the time to pass more quickly. Standing by the window and anxiously observing the planes coming in, a woman in a small group struggled to keep back the tears as time for her seemed to have slowed down, if not actually stopped. Here and there were people who were alone — some walking with a clear sense of direction and purpose, others strolling along while drinking in the scenes of the airport drama. Occasionally a lone traveler, unkempt and with a troubled countenance, wandered through, seemingly undirected, going anywhere and maybe nowhere.

These scenes I had become accustomed to in my travels in

many parts of the world. I routinely smiled at the joy of those awaiting the return of a loved one and felt some emotion for those bidding farewell and also some concern for the lone and troubled traveler.

One morning, having said my good-byes with little emotion since the separation would be very brief, I began the familiar walk down the concourse to Gate B-6. With ticket in hand and holding the strap attached to my small suitcase on wheels, I maneuvered into the crowd, seemingly carried forward without any effort on my part. It was a rather strange sensation, but since the crowd was moving in the direction I wanted to go, I felt no resistance as I was drawn into the flow.

Just a few steps ahead of me I noticed a young mother with a baby tucked securely under one arm and a heavy bag weighing her down on the other shoulder. I pushed forward, thinking I might be able to offer some assistance. When I got next to her, I observed her concern. Hidden down between the passengers were three little children, all hanging onto their mother's skirt, crowding against her legs, and making it difficult for her to walk and maintain her balance in the crowd. She bent over in an effort to communicate with her little flock. By now I was within hearing distance of this anxious traveler, and between the loud voice over the intercom giving directions and announcing departing flights, I heard this mother say, in an anxious tone, "Listen to me. We must take hold of hands and hang on tight."

At that very moment I felt a small hand slip into mine. I held it gently for only a second or two, and then it was quickly withdrawn. The little child had responded. It was my hand that happened to be close, and she took hold. For just a moment I felt an overwhelming sense of responsibility for this little child I didn't even know and concern for a mother I had never met.

I wondered, *What does it mean to take hold of hands and hang on tight?* If a child or an adult, a fellow traveler, were to take my hand, would I lead them to board the plane that would take them safely home? How much assistance can one traveler give in helping another along the journey, especially a young and inexperienced traveler?

In nature's miracles we see a community spirit, concern for one another, played out in a most remarkable way. Animals helping one another overcome great odds, driving off enemies, surviving seasonal changes, and protecting their young. Animals, like people, exhibit competitive instincts, but they are also balanced by another inherent drive. There is the natural instinct to take care of self, but there is also a second instinct: to get together. It has been said that the idea of community is as vital as the breath of life. Zoologists have found that even tadpoles are deeply influenced by social needs. A solitary tadpole can regenerate an injured part of its body very slowly, but if it is given the dimly sensed comradeship of fellow tadpoles, its healing powers speed up almost miraculously.

The care and concern and righteous influence of faithful Saints will overcome the odds for us and for others in this challenging, threatening, and otherwise unsettling time.

President Spencer W. Kimball taught that the influence of righteous women would be critical during the winding-up scenes on this earth before the second coming of the Savior. ("Privileges and Responsibilities of Sisters," *Ensign*, November 1978, p. 103.) This is our time to be a righteous influence. There are righteous women throughout the world with whom we need to unite. We need not wait for a calling but can be anxiously engaged of our own free will.

I do not wish to make anyone feel encumbered or burdened, but to point out that little things can mean so very much. Doctrine and Covenants 64:33 says simply, "Wherefore, be not weary in well-doing, for ye are laying the foundation of a great work. And out of small things proceedeth that which is great."

In the April 1990 general conference, President Thomas S. Monson, quoted our prophet, President Ezra Taft Benson, who said, "We must dedicate our strength to serving the needs, rather than the fears, of the world." Then President Monson added, "Perhaps never in history has the need for cooperation, understanding and goodwill among all people—and nations and individuals alike—been so urgent as today" (*Ensign*, May 1990, pp. 4–5.)

Others who spoke in the same session reminded us of the importance of caring for one another. "Service helps us overcome selfishness and sin," said Elder Derek A. Cuthbert. "[It] helps us cleanse ourselves and become purified and sanctified." Elder Hans B. Ringger reminded us that we must "live the example of the good Samaritan, who was free of prejudice and excuses and therefore truly loved his neighbor." And Elder Neal A. Maxwell stated, "When, for the moment, we ourselves are not being stretched on a particular cross, we ought to be at the foot of someone else's—full of empathy and proffering spiritual refreshment."

The hymn "As Sisters in Zion" includes the line, "How vast is our purpose, how broad is our mission." (*Hymns*, no. 309.) What is our responsibility to bring relief within our own homes, our neighborhood, our community, our country, our world? Do we confine ourselves to our own comfort zones? Can we offer relief from rejection and abuse, relief from loneliness and isolation? Do we see service when it is close to home, across the street, down the aisle in the marketplace? Can we unite to bring relief from the devastation of drugs and alcohol and the addicting power of pornography? Can we bring relief from illiteracy and poverty and extend relief not only to the homeless but also to those in spiritual darkness, depression, despair? Our opportunity and responsibility to cheer and to bless in humanity's name beckons us to service.

To cheer and to bless in humanity's name takes us beyond our immediate neighborhood. We must tear down fences and walls and build bridges. Recently I was invited to participate in a meeting of the National Women's Leadership Task Force, a coalition of thirty women working to stamp out pornography. As you read the following from my notes of that meeting, ask yourself if you would be willing to participate with these women in that cause.

"We must have a theological and ethical base. The New Testament refers to the beloved community where each one has dignity, value, and worth."

"This is a calling," one woman commented. "Yes, because we are Christian women, but also because we are citizens. This problem erodes that covenant base which is the fiber of our republic. This problem unleashes and distorts human passion."

Another woman admitted to having misjudged someone. "I saw her as being different," she said. "I had an ally and I mistook her."

"Broaden the base," a woman urged. "One woman can be helpful, ten women influential, one hundred women powerful, one thousand women invincible. Train women to interact in the process, to work with excellence and respect, integrity and balance."

Then another woman said quietly, "I've been praying to get out of it. God is keeping us in it to do something about it."

"I feel the Lord put this all together," the leader of the group said. "If you let in the light, he will bring in what else is needed."

Alexis de Tocqueville was quoted: "Righteous women in their circle of influence beginning in the home can turn the world around."

"When committed women are singing off the same song sheet," one woman said, "we can make a difference. We need to promote virtue. That is the bottom line. The Lord impressed upon my spirit that God will give voice to women who are standing for righteousness. I believe we are here, placed at a point in human history, by God's design. My heart longs for the day when all women everywhere will stand up and speak out for righteousness that affects our homes, our communities, our nation, but most of all our families." Then she emphasized, "Before we do anything, however, we must have prayer support. This evil is out of the pits of hell. When the women of this nation become mobilized in righteous causes and converted into votes, when we put our heads together, pray together, put our shoulders to the wheel, we can turn this thing around. We have been called to be righteous women. Think of all you have accomplished and then ask yourself, what does God want me to do now?"

The chairman closed the meeting with this thought: "The Lord bless you and keep you and use you all for his glory. Amen."

It is not enough to strive only to promote what is good. Must we not also accept responsibility to unite our efforts and extend our influence to eradicate the bad? I would like to tell you of a Relief Society in Las Vegas that determined to break with tradition. Rather than the usual Relief Society birthday social, nine wards united to research their community. They identified twenty major projects that could affect, protect, and guard the homes in their community. Each of the nine wards chose one activity. The sisters from one ward participated in projects leading to the dedication of the temple in that area. Another group focused their concern on the telephone directory, which contained twenty-five pages advertising escort services (that is, women for hire); the pornographic language and pictures in the ads defiled the homes they were placed in. While some sisters blessed their community by participating in the completion of a temple in their midst, others blessed their community by uniting their forces to remove pornographic material from their homes.

Our labors are needed on both fronts, to promote the good and eradicate the bad. Often we hesitate, concerned that if we take a stand we will be criticized. But we need to take that risk; we need to articulate our values. There is a proper framework for voicing our opinion. When I went to Washington, D.C., to present a paper to the Meese Commission Against Pornography, I confess it was not comfortable. I was there with representatives from many organizations, including *Playboy* and other magazines. Sometimes taking a stand simply is not comfortable. But I think we can be a righteous influence with dignity, with propriety, with clarity, and in support of constitutional procedures, though not with tolerance for things we know to be wrong.

Sometimes Mormon women fear that it may not be appropriate for them to enter a political arena even in issues that endanger the home; however, the assignments that I have received from our priesthood leaders tell me that we may not have the luxury to sit on the sidelines and hope that someone else will stand up and speak out for what we believe.

"Out of small things proceedeth that which is great." In a stake in Draper, Utah, the stake Relief Society president gathered women together and, with quilting frames border to border in the entire cultural hall, they made two hundred quilts to cover the beds in the Primary Children's Medical Center. Each sister may have felt that her small contribution would not make much difference, but I think of the words of Mother Teresa: "I always say I'm a little pencil in the hands of God. He does the thinking. He does the writing. He does everything—and it's really hard—sometimes it's a broken pencil. He has to sharpen it a little more. But be a little instrument in His hands so that He can use you any time, anywhere. . . . We have only to say Yes to Him." (*Love: A Fruit Always in Season,* San Francisco: Ignatius Press, 1987, p. 243.)

When are the seeds for that kind of ministering planted and in what settings are they nourished? Among the Young Women Values is Good Works, which states, "We will nurture others and build the kingdom through righteous service." A letter from one young woman provides a prescription for all of us. It describes the steps and displays the fruits of service, which blesses both the server and the one being served. She writes: "Last year in my junior high school year I set a goal in Good Works: to try to help someone in some little way every day, whether it was something that I did or just said or an example that I set. I decided to do this prayerfully, so every day before I went to school I prayed and I asked Heavenly Father, let me have the influence of the Spirit to know what I should do or say."

She reports that these small acts of service changed not only her attitude about herself but also her attitude toward others. "I began to see how everything we do affects others. . . . I began to feel better about myself and at the same time more humble.

97

. . . Through my actions I began to have a different outlook on all my brothers and sisters. Everyone should be treated with respect. Through my daily efforts I feel as though I am beginning to understand what love can really be."

A feeling of wanting to reach out beyond ourselves falls like gentle rain on parched soil on those days when we may feel useless or worthless or unfulfilled or maybe even bored or lonely. It answers our deeper spiritual needs. With charity in our hearts, we can go out beyond the borders of our own comfort zone; we can let our influence be felt for righteousness in circles where we may not initially be familiar or at ease. Charity is the key. A prayerful heart gives the direction.

When we learn to listen to the Spirit in answer to our prayers, our service becomes customized by the Spirit, and we will do things that we might not otherwise have known to do. At Christmastime one year I talked to a widow on her doorstep. "My freezer is full of goodies," she said. "And obviously I don't need them," she added with a laugh, as she looked down at her expanding waistline. Then she commented wistfully, "But you don't really see the lights on Temple square unless you go there with a family." She would have traded all of the cakes and cookies for such an invitation. When we seek direction of the Spirit, our labors will be more meaningful—and maybe even require less effort.

The value and far-reaching effects of our service, however small, have nothing to do with our age or material wealth. They have to do with our willingness to give of our time and be led by the Spirit. Many lives will be healed and blessed when we reach out in a spirit of love and concern. I think of a little girl who visited a neighbor's house where her little friend had died. "Why did you go?" asked her father. "To comfort her mother," she said. "What could you do to comfort her?" "I climbed into her lap and cried with her," she said.

Our "Jericho Roads" may be just across the street, but they are there for each of us as we travel toward home.

The Prophet Joseph Smith taught that life is like a huge

wagon wheel. Like the revolving wheel, all of us at some time will find ourselves on the bottom, needing someone literally to pull us up. But as life evolves, there will be times when we are on top of the wheel and can reach down and help lift others up.

As the children of Israel journeyed from the wilderness of Sin, Moses provided the leadership and direction while Joshua fought with Amalek. "Joshua did as Moses had said, and fought with Amalek: and Moses, Aaron, and Hur went up to the top of the hill. And it came to pass, when Moses held up his hand, that Israel prevailed: and when he let down his hand, Amalek prevailed. But Moses' hands were heavy; and they took a stone, and put it under him, and he sat thereon; and Aaron and Hur stayed up his hands, the one on the one side, and the other on the other side; and his hands were steady until the going down of the sun." (Exodus 17:10–12).

May we remember always the counsel given by the young mother to her little children in the busy airport with crowds of people going many different directions: "We must take hold of hands and hang on tight." Let us become a community of saints bound together by our common goals and our eternal relationship as brothers and sisters in the gospel of Jesus Christ.

CHAPTER 11

Finding Joy in Service

D o you remember the story of the Little Red Hen, and how industrious, ambitious, independent, and self-reliant she was? Do you recall how she had a wonderful plan in mind that began by trying to get her friends to help her plant a few grains of wheat? As the story goes, she clucked around the barnyard asking, "Who will help me plant these grains of wheat?" And each of her friends responded the same way. "Not I," said the goose. "Not I," said the pig. "Not I," said the dog. "Then I will plant them myself," said the Little Red Hen. And she did.

She asked for help each step of the way. She asked for help with watering the wheat, tending and caring for it, cutting it, and finally grinding it into flour. Always the answer was the same: "Not I."

One fall morning the Little Red Hen got up early to make the flour into bread. She decided to give her friends one last chance to help, but the answer was still the same. "Not I," said the goose. "Not I," said the pig. "Not I," said the dog.

By now she must have been quite upset at having done all the work by herself, but she went ahead and baked a loaf of bread without their help. While she was laboring alone, she may have been thinking about her friends. Were they really friends after all? Why didn't they help? Didn't they know she needed them? Weren't they interested in her plan? Didn't they care about her? To offset her disappointment, perhaps she said, "I don't care. I don't need them anyway. I can do it by myself."

As delicious aromas from the baking bread filled the air, she anticipated that moment of taking it from the oven and eating it by herself, maybe with peanut butter and jam. Can't you just see her anticipating each animal's answer to her question, "Who will help me eat the bread"? Each one enthusiastically responded, "Oh, I will, I will." By now the Little Red Hen had her chance to get even with them. "You will?" she said indignantly. "I did all the work by myself. Now I'm going to eat it all by myself." And according to the story, that is exactly what she did. "It was only fair," she must have told herself. After all, she had done all the work.

How might it have been if, in the very beginning, the Little Red Hen had explained to her friends what she wanted to have happen? What if she had told them she had a plan for a wonderful event in just a few months, a celebration to which they were all invited? And what if she had called it a celebration of friendship, a time of breaking bread and eating it with jam and jelly? And that in addition, there would be several times before the party when they would be able to get together as friends and work together and contribute to this great celebration? Suppose, because of her enthusiasm, so many wanted to participate in the planting that she had to get more grain to plant because no one would want to be left out. As a result of everyone's help, there would be so much bread baked that they could write notes of love and deliver bread to everyone, not only in the barnyard but also down the lane and across the field.

In the beginning, maybe the Little Red Hen really couldn't get anyone to help with the project until it was time to eat the bread. But even then, what if she had shared the bread she had worked so hard to make? When it was all eaten, think of the friendships that would have been made. Wouldn't that have been more fun than eating the bread alone and muttering to herself, "It serves them right"?

The Little Red Hen knew what she wanted to do—she

wanted to make bread. She knew the steps and the processes needed to complete the project. But she did not fully consider what she wanted to have happen as a result of her work. What if she had thought more about how to reach out to her friends and to involve them in ways that would bring them together, where they might discover the talents and uniqueness of each other's contribution? And what if, in the process, they came to value each other's differences and rely on each other, learn from each other, respect each other, build closer friendships, and have fun together?

Another familiar story also takes place in the barnyard, but this one is quite different. In *Charlotte's Web* by E. B. White, poor Wilbur the Pig had no friends at all. According to the story, he felt so "friendless, dejected, and hungry, he threw himself down in the manure and sobbed." Have you ever had a Wilbur day? It can hurt a lot inside if you feel you don't have even one friend. But in the story, Charlotte the Spider came to Wilbur's rescue. She asked, "Do you want a friend, Wilbur? I'll be a friend to you. I've watched you all day and I like you." Not only did Charlotte express her feelings for Wilbur, which must have given him some hope, but far into the night while the other animals slept, she also worked on a web that would literally save his life. She worked many nights to rescue him from the danger of being sold and ending up as bacon in the local meat market. Finally, just before Charlotte was going to die, as spiders do, Wilbur shared his feelings for her. "Oh, Charlotte," he said. "To think that when I first met you I thought you were cruel and bloodthirsty! Why did you do all this for me? I don't deserve it. I've never done anything for you."

"You have been my friend," replied Charlotte. "That in itself is a tremendous thing."

"Well," said Wilbur, "I'm no good at making speeches. I haven't got your gift for words. But you have saved me, Charlotte, and I would gladly give my life for you. I really would." Through her good works, Charlotte had become Wilbur's best friend. She cared enough for him that she used her special skills to serve him and eventually save his life.

Just think of the lessons that Charlotte could have taught the Little Red Hen and the other animals about service, friendship, and caring for one another, and about good works, even working through the night to accomplish an important project, maybe even to save someone's life. Doing good works means to nurture others, to care about others, to serve others, and to build friendships that bring joy and rewards and great happiness. When we are seeking only for our own interests, it is quite possible to become rather selfish, but when we follow the Golden Rule and do unto others as we would have them do unto us, we learn to put aside our own desires and reach out to others. And in the end, we discover that we have gained all that we really wanted and even more.

When Jesus lived on the earth, he taught the people things that would help them eventually become like him. One of his messages was, "Let your light so shine before men, that they may see your good works, and glorify your Father which is in heaven." (Matthew 5:16.) This instruction tells us not only what we should do to follow Christ but also why: to bring glory and honor to our Father in heaven.

When we, as members of The Church of Jesus Christ of Latter-day Saints, went into the waters of baptism, we covenanted or promised our Heavenly Father that we would help one another. Each time we partake of the sacred emblems of the sacrament, we renew our baptismal covenant with him that we will always remember him and that we will keep his commandments. When we do this, we have the promise that we can always have his Spirit to be with us. During the Last Supper, just before Jesus died on the cross so that each one of us could return to our Father, he gave a very important commandment to his apostles, one that was for all of us, for all time. He said, "This is my commandment, that ye love one another, as I have loved you." (John 15:12.)

Consider the far-reaching effects of the service performed

by a young woman in Arizona who was working on her Laurel project. Robyn decided she wanted to help organize a reunion for members of her father's family, many of whom were not LDS. She prayed about it and received a good feeling that this was what she was supposed to do.

Robyn decided the best place to have the reunion would be Southern California, since many of the family members lived in California. She called long-distance to her father's cousin in Palos Verdes Estates, south of Los Angeles, and asked if they could have the reunion at his home. He agreed, and together they set the date and worked out some of the details. Then she called another relative to get the names and addresses of family members.

Using her family's home computer, Robyn prepared a letter announcing the reunion and asking family members to cut off a coupon at the bottom and mail it back if they were interested in such a function. The response was overwhelming—letters and phone calls flooded in. Every single person responded and was excited about the reunion.

During the next four months, Robyn busily planned the reunion. She communicated with all fifty-three family members every month, giving them details of the reunion, giving them food assignments, and even sending them a list of all the names and addresses and a map showing them how to get to the reunion. She paid for the mailings with her own wages from a part-time job.

The reunion was very successful. Sixty-five family members came, some from great distances, and the spirit of love flowed through all the activities. Before dinner, everyone gathered for the first time as a complete family and had family prayer together, offered by an uncle who is a minister in another faith.

Robyn's mother wrote, "There was a very special bonding that occurred the day of the reunion, and everyone recognized that Robyn had been the catalyst. In fact, before everyone left to go home, they assembled and presented Robyn with a poster they had worked on during the day. On the poster was drawn a family tree showing how everyone at the reunion fit in, and alongside their names, each person had written a special note to Robyn, thanking her for all her efforts. Since the reunion, we have received many warm notes and phone calls expressing love and saying how wonderful the reunion was. Many wonderful seeds of the gospel were planted that day."

But that isn't all. A few months later Robyn's grandfather passed away. At ninety, he was the eldest member of the family and lived next door to Robyn and her family. Because of the list Robyn had gathered for the reunion, her parents were able to contact relatives in a matter of hours. They decided to have just a graveside service, since few members of the family lived in that area. Though the grandfather was not a member of the Church, they asked their bishop to conduct.

Imagine their surprise when, the night before the services, family members from several states began arriving. There were so many that the simple graveside service quickly turned into a funeral service with speakers and musical numbers. The relatives, none of them LDS, were deeply touched by the service, and some wonderful missionary moments occurred as a result.

Perhaps the most wonderful spin-off, her mother wrote, is the changes that have occurred in Robyn as a result of this experience. "She is confident, outgoing, and we have discovered a hidden talent—an amazing gift of organization."

I wonder how Robyn felt as the result of her Laurel project. I wonder how each member of her family felt about Robyn's efforts to bring them all together. I wonder how Heavenly Father felt about the part Robyn played in helping to build, strengthen, and bond her family together, not only now but hopefully in the eternities.

Good Works, one of the Young Women values, states, "I will nurture others and build the kingdom through righteous service." Good works may not always be a major project. It might be accomplished with what President Spencer W. Kimball called small acts of service. He taught us that "when we concern ourselves more with others, there is less time to be concerned with ourselves. In the midst of the miracle of serving, there is the promise of Jesus, that by losing ourselves, we find ourselves. (See Matt. 10:39.) Not only do we 'find' ourselves in terms of acknowledging guidance in our lives, but the more we serve our fellowmen in appropriate ways, the more substance there is to our souls. We become more significant individuals as we serve others. We become more substantive as we serve others—indeed, it is easier to 'find' ourselves because there is so much more of us to find!" ("Small Acts of Service," *Ensign,* December 1974, p. 2.)

Sometimes because of circumstances it may seem that there is very little that we can do to help others. This is not the case at all. Young Erika Monson teaches us something about letting our light shine under any circumstance. Erika learned that a two-year-old girl, Kirstin, was fighting for her life. Every effort was being made to locate bone marrow compatible with Kirstin's in the desperate hope that a transplant could be made to save this little girl's life. Responding to a concern not only for the little girl but also for her family, Erika wrote the following letter to Kirstin's parents:

"Dear Brother and Sister Doxey: How is your family doing? My name is Erika Monson. I am from Ely, Nevada. I am in Primary Children's Hospital and getting better. I know how hard things are for you and your family even though I'm thirteen. I hope that your daughter Kirstin is lucky and finds the right donor so she can hopefully live to be a young woman. If I was old enough to donate and wasn't on medicine for my liver, I would see if I matched your daughter's type. If so, I would do everything to make it so she would be able to live. I hope and pray for the best for your family. Love, Erika Monson."

While Erika Monson faced her own struggles for life and health, she reached outside herself to empathize with someone else. Elder Neal A. Maxwell tells us that when we can have concern for the welfare of another, even while we are suffering with our own problems, we are true disciples of Christ. We are following in his path and responding to his invitation, "Come, follow me." When we learn to listen to the promptings of the Spirit, we discover a natural desire, a yearning, to reach out to other people.

Heather, a young woman, writes about her desire to serve: "I want to be the one little light in the darkness so that not only I will survive, but maybe my friends will too. My friends are mostly nonmembers because of the small number of Mormons who go to my high school. The thing I really want to commit to doing is the very most good I can. Although there are times when I am not off the strait and narrow, I may not be dead center on that path either. Then I'll get upset with myself because I know I can do better. Starting right now, I'd like to commit to be the best I can be—not to just not be bad, but to reach out and help others all that I can. I feel really inspired to straighten out my life. I really promise the Lord that I'll keep these commitments I've made."

Karen, Robyn, Erika, and Heather are just a few examples of hundreds of young women throughout the world who are "nurturing others and building the kingdom through righteous service," as stated in the Young Women Values.

In the Book of Mormon the writings of King Benjamin help us understand the sacredness of service, the privilege and blessing of service, and the magnitude of even our smallest efforts: "When ye are in the service of your fellow beings ye are only in the service of your God." (Mosiah 2:17.)

Most good works that are performed daily come as the result of an individual responding to the desire to serve, but there are also groups, classes, and teams of young people who perform major tasks through well-planned service projects. Some time ago I read with excitement a newspaper report about a group of young men and women who, while participating in a youth conference, converged on the little community of Wales, Utah. There they erected a chain-link fence around the town cemetery, painted picnic tables and playground equipment at the town park, cleared vacant lots, tore down old buildings, hauled away debris, and even laid down a cement sidewalk and patio for an elderly couple. The youths invited the townspeople to be their special guests at a watermelon bust around a huge bonfire one evening, and a talent show, barbecued turkey dinner, and dance another evening. "It was one grand get-together," a resident said. (*Deseret News,* June 25, 1987.)

A group in Glendora, California, participated in a service project during their spring break the week before Easter. Every day that week two groups of young men and young women, accompanied by their leaders, traveled to downtown Los Angeles, some twenty-five miles from their homes, to spend three hours helping to set up, serve, and clean up for the meals served at a skid-row mission. They also sorted clothing, wrapped five thousand plastic utensils in napkins for the Easter meal, and prepared more than 150 Easter baskets filled with donated items, such as toothbrushes, toothpaste, combs, soap, and Easter candies. On Easter they helped serve a special meal to five thousand needy people on a downtown street.

According to a newspaper report of the project, "A high point for many was singing to the homeless at the Sunday street meal. Strains of 'I Am a Child of God,' 'Because I Have Been Given Much,' and 'Love One Another' brought a quiet hush to the otherwise noisy street scene and tears to the eyes of singers and audience alike." (*Church News,* April 28, 1990.)

Our acts of service may be large or small, lengthy or brief, public or private, but when we serve in a spirit of love and sincere concern for the welfare and happiness of another, the Spirit of the Lord is felt and the Lord can work through us to bless others. Love expressed through service can bring light where there is darkness, hope where there is despair, and repentance where there is transgression.

To young women of the Church, I say: Make a commitment today to do some small act of service for someone every day. In days and years to come, precious memories will return again and again as you think of the wonderful feelings you had as a result of your Good Works experience. On those occasions words similar to these might come to your mind:

"Come, ye blessed of my Father, inherit the kingdom prepared for you from the foundation of the world: for you let your light so shine that others were blessed by your good works, and you glorified your Father in heaven."

You may ask, "But when did I help glorify my Father in heaven? What did I do that was so important?"

The answer will come to your mind: "When you reached out to help another, when you had the moral courage to stand for truth and righteousness even when it was very difficult, when you comforted the lonely, when you tended a child, when you helped strengthen a testimony . . . "

And then you will remember the words of the Savior, "Inasmuch as ye have done it unto one of the least of these my brethren, ye have done it unto me." (See Matthew 5:16; 25:34–40.)

CHAPTER 12

"She's My Sister"

Two sisters sat close to each other on the leather-covered sofa in the outer office, whispering words of encouragement to each other. "You can go first if you want to," Linda offered her younger sister. Mary was thoughtful for a moment before replying, "I really think you should go first. It will be better that way." Then, with increased intensity in her voice, she touched her sister's arm and added, "Please be first."

At that moment the door to the inner office opened and the secretary invited either of the applicants to come in for the job interview. Linda exchanged a quick glance with her sister and received the necessary encouragement to be first. With outward dignity and poise, but with her heart pounding a fast, unsteady rhythm, she entered and sat on the chair beside the desk. She listened intently to the requirements, the expectations, the opportunities, and the benefits of the job.

With increasing confidence, Linda related her experiences and preparation that would be of particular value in the work the employer had just outlined. Her excitement for the possibility of employment was evident. With this part-time job on campus she would be able to continue her education, pay back her loan, and live in the dormitory with her friends and her sister. It all seemed too good to be true, and yet there was a possibility.

Then, with a prayer in her heart, she waited. The interview apparently completed, the employer glanced out the window thoughtfully before turning to face Linda. Finally she asked, "And if I hire you for the job, what about your sister?"

Like air rapidly escaping from an inflated balloon, Linda's enthusiasm quickly slipped away. There was only one job opening! Somehow the advertisement in the university paper had given her the impression that there were many. Now she was in competition with her sister for the same job.

With great effort, she managed to hide her disappointment and regain some of her original enthusiasm. In that moment, her personal interests were set aside. As if having prepared for this opportunity over many years, she began enumerating Mary's many qualities with the conviction of a true advocate. With both hands outstretched to provide additional emphasis, she took up the cause for her sister. "If there is only one opening, just one job, please talk to Mary, my sister." As she rose to leave, she added, "Mary worked long, long hours while I was on my mission. She saved every penny she could so that when I returned we could both come to school. I know she sacrificed a lot of things just for me, just so we could be together. My sister did that all for me." Her voice softened, and tears filled her eyes. "I wouldn't even be here if it weren't for Mary. When you meet her, you'll know what I mean."

Regaining her composure, Linda returned to the outer office, where Mary was waiting. She whispered, "Good luck!" and they exchanged places. Inside the employer's office the same routine procedures for job interviews were covered and the same details were presented. Mary's enthusiasm was equal to that of Linda's—a fresh, unsophisticated, honest eagerness to obtain part-time employment. Then, sensitive to the reality of the situation, she asked, "What about my sister?" Somewhat hesitantly, the employer confirmed what Mary had feared. "There is only one job opening at this time," was the response.

Like a faithful evangelist, Mary took up her sister's cause. "My sister is the one you will want," she said. "She's a returned missionary and has the ability to meet people much better than

I. Everyone loves Linda. If there is only one opening, please consider Linda."

The deep feelings of love, concern, and loyalty these two young women expressed for each other interested the employer more than the immediate task of filling a job. Neither knew of the other's advocacy. At the conclusion of the interview she asked Mary to remain seated, then stepped to the door and invited Linda in. The two girls sat side by side, obviously renewed by the strength of being together. The formality of the interviews had been replaced now by a spirit of expectation as each one wanted most what she thought was best for the other. They listened intently while the employer carefully, and with obvious emotion, unfolded the moving details of the past hour.

When Mary heard the details of Linda's interview, she bowed her head and reached over to clasp her sister's hand. Tears filled their eyes as Mary leaned close to Linda and murmured, "But it's no more than you would have done for me if I'd been called on a mission."

The employer then related the details of Mary's interview while Linda learned how her sister had set aside her own personal desires. Linda's feelings of love and appreciation now demanded even further expression. "Mary has more love in her heart than anyone I've ever met," she said. "She has an unselfish quality of giving and being able to serve others willingly. It's the spirit of Christ, and she's got it more than I have. That's what I'm striving to develop."

Mary interrupted her sister. "But you gave yourself totally on your mission. Let me tell you, you did!" Then, turning to the employer, she spoke with deep emotion. "You see, Linda is three years older than I am, and she has paved the way for me through all the difficult times when I was younger. I haven't reached her height yet, but she stands by me all the way."

Linda, smiling through her tears, responded, "She's my sister. I always will."

CHAPTER 13

"This Is All
the Money I Have"

The kindly old man didn't go outside as much anymore, and he didn't cross the street over to the Gardners' home as he used to. During the winter he had been there many times, not only to the Gardners' home but also to the homes of neighbors up and down both sides of the street. After a heavy snowstorm he was usually out at the crack of dawn to clear the snow from driveways, providing a happy surprise in the early morning hours for grateful neighbors and friends. In the summertime he carefully arranged selected vegetables in baskets and carried them across the street to share with his neighbors. But it was not his vegetables that made him so popular with the children so much as the sweets he always had for them when they came around to the back door. His dear wife, restricted to a wheelchair, insisted on including "something sweet for the children" in their weekly shopping list.

Another winter season was slipping away, yielding to the warm sun of springtime. With this season came other signs of ebbing away. The old man's garden had been planted with much difficulty this year. He tended it less often than usual, but enough, he hoped, to assure a good harvest that he might share one last time with his neighbors and friends. His good health was gone. His service to his friends was now greatly restricted. Some days were difficult and some were long for both him and his wife. "The very worst thing about being sick," he explained, "isn't the pain so much as it is the feeling of being so useless."

115

He swallowed hard to keep the tears under control and forced a smile into the careworn lines on his face.

Across the street at the home of the Gardners, young Elizabeth, only seven and a half years old, had acquired a keen sense of concern for others. In her family, when anyone had a problem or felt unhappy, they discovered little ways to cheer each other up. Over her few short years, this child had observed her faithful mother find time to wipe a tear, heal a wound with a kiss, and listen to the never-ending account of a child who needed her attention. It was not just within the busy yet happy setting of her home that Elizabeth witnessed this activity. The same concern was expressed by her mother in many ways beyond her home, up and down the street to those in need, as the children distributed hot cinnamon rolls to many, or a dinner for a family on a special occasion.

One day Elizabeth left her home quietly without telling anyone what was on her mind or in her hand. She looked both ways, then crossed the street. She was not carrying hot cinnamon rolls from her mother's kitchen as she had often done before. She came carrying her own treasures. She walked quietly through the carport and made her way under the balcony to the back door with the little glass window in it. She rang the bell at the home of the kind old man and his dear crippled wife, then quickly hurried to hide behind the large bush of Oregon grape.

Inside the home the old couple looked at each other and wondered who would be calling at this hour. The man, with some effort, eased himself up from his big chair, stretched his back before taking a step, then shuffled toward the door. As he opened the door, his wife strained to hear a voice that she might identify. There were birds in the feeder that he attended to each day, but no one was in sight. He stepped out to look around, looking first one way, then the other, but there was no sign of anyone.

As he turned to go back inside, he noticed a torn piece of paper on the step by the door. It was a piece of newsprint, the kind he had seen children carry home from school sticking out

116

of their books and sometimes falling along the way. The paper had writing on it, and on top of the paper were two coins – one nickel and one quarter. Steadying one hand on his leg, he reached to the ground to pick up the note and the money. He could see that a message had been printed by a child.

By now his wife was calling, "Ted, is someone there?" She called again, "Ted?"

He shuffled back into the living room. "No one was there," he said in a quiet voice.

"Then what do you have in your hand?"

"Someone has been here," he explained. "Look at this."

He sat beside his wife on the couch and together, straining to see through their glasses, they read these few words: "Dear Mr. and Mrs. Greene, You are very dear friends of ours, you are always nice to us. Here is something you might need. From Elizabeth Gardner." Words barely hanging on the bottom of the edge of the page completed the message, "This is all the money I have."

Holding the paper in one hand, he opened his other hand to show his wife. There in the palm of a trembling hand lay the nickel and the quarter. "All the money she has," he whispered, "a mite." His wife removed her glasses to wipe a tear from her eye and brushed a lock of gray hair from her forehead. "Like a widow's mite," he added. Together they sat holding the small piece of paper and two coins while they thought of a plan.

Walking with the help of a cane, Brother Greene made his way over to the Gardners' home, knocked on the door, and asked to speak to Elizabeth. She came to the door, her chin buried in her neck while she looked at the floor. The old man stooped over to wrap her in one of his arms while he steadied himself with his cane. Giving her a gentle hug, he thanked her for all she had done to make him and his wife so happy. The child smiled and looked up at her mother, who was now standing at her side, curious to know what her daughter had done. Elizabeth then told her mother about her visit to the Greenes.

"In our family we think of little things to do for or give to

117

people if they are feeling bad," Sister Gardner said. "We write notes to each other and leave little things like a cookie or a piece of candy. One time one of my sisters carved a little heart out of soap to go with a note she wrote to me when I was feeling unhappy." In a matter-of-fact tone Elizabeth added, "I got the idea from what we do in our family, and I decided to take it outside of my family. I could see that Brother and Sister Greene were getting old, and I thought they might need to pay hospital bills or something." Then in a happy tone she concluded, "so I gave them all the money I had."

Now Brother Greene felt not so useless after all. There were still lessons to learn and people to serve. The following Sunday the aged man and the sensitive child visited with the ward clerk. "We'd like to make a contribution," they said, "a contribution of one nickel and one quarter to help build the Jordan River Temple." The clerk was somewhat surprised. He was aware that each of them had made contributions individually, but the combined donation was a curious entry on the official form.

Brother Greene asked the clerk if they could have duplicate receipts so both he and Elizabeth would have one, but the clerk explained that only one receipt could be made. It was decided that she would get it.

"I was so anxious for it," she later explained, "and it seemed like weeks before I got it. The day I received it, I took it over and showed it to Brother and Sister Greene. Brother Greene took me by the hand and led me over to the wall by his radio and showed me my letter, which he had framed."

A few months later Brother Greene passed away. As his treasures were being tucked away, the framed picture was removed from its place on the wall. Taped to it were a nickel and a quarter, reminders of the generous gift of a little girl who had given him all the money she had.

KEEPING
IN TOUCH

CHAPTER 14

Calling Home

H ello! Hello! I'm sorry I can't hear you!" I shouted into the telephone. Hanging up the phone, I searched anxiously for another one somewhere away from the noise and commotion of the people from many lands, speaking different languages, going in every direction, at the Heathrow Airport in London, England. That tower of Babel incident really caused a problem, I thought, as I observed one traveler unsuccessfully seeking information in a language foreign to another, followed by a gesture they both could translate: a shrug of the shoulders meaning, "I don't understand." They could hear each other all right, but it was obvious the message was not getting through.

Mine was a different problem. I couldn't hear. Trying to hold back the tears and feeling so far away from home, I located another telephone down the concourse. I had been in the British Isles on an assignment for over three weeks. I had planned to take the train from Stoke-on-Trent to London for my 4:15 P.M. flight to Los Angeles. If I could just get that far, I thought, I could even walk the rest of the way to Utah if necessary. Due to a difference in the train schedules from weekday to Sunday, however, I missed my connection for the 4:15 flight by twenty minutes. The plane headed for home was in the air but I was on the ground. I needed to call home. I wanted to be home. An emptiness crowded in, and I felt sick—homesick.

Locating another telephone, I read the instructions carefully, then once again dialed the international number printed on my telephone credit card. First a number, followed by the letter M, then three more numbers grouped together, plus three more, then four numbers, and finally the number eight. Twelve numbers in all, plus the letter M. I waited anxiously, hoping for a clear connection as I heard the call going through. How does this magic of communication across continents, under the ocean, in outer space, take place?

In my state of homesickness, I returned in my mind to my home when I was a child. I could see the calendar on the wall with our telephone number clearly printed at the bottom. My mother owned and operated a little country store, and each year she gave her customers and friends a calendar with a different picture for each season. But the information printed on the bottom was always the same. It could hardly be considered advertising since there was no competitor, but the information was important and seemed to lend prestige to our small business. It read in black letters:

Greene's General Store
Groceries, Dry Goods, Novelties
Glenwood, Alberta, Phone #3.

I didn't need a telephone calling card to remember #3.

The phone, like a large box, hung on the wall with a silver-colored receiver you held to your ear. We could pick up the receiver almost any time of the day and hear any one of ten people whom we knew and loved exchanging valuable information. A party line, we called it. Sister Woodruff would be giving a recipe for baked beans or some other dish to Sister Glines, who missed Relief Society the week when the recipe was shared. And if you didn't get in on the beginning of the conversation, it was never a problem for Sister Woodruff to repeat it. Communication was wonderful in those days until after six o'clock, when the switchboard, located in my grandmother's house, was closed for the day and the operator did not come on duty again until eight o'clock the following morning. In the case of an emergency, a loud siren-like sound could be heard anywhere in the house and would bring someone running to take the call.

Surely this was an emergency, I thought as I waited in the phone booth in London. Someone will answer. I anxiously waited as the telephone rang six, seven, eight times. Oh, if I could just get through to one of those old-time operators of long ago who answered "Information please" with such feeling and concern, I knew I'd feel better. She could always report on where you might locate any person in the town, what they were doing, and when they might be home if they didn't answer their phone.

Our operator could always answer our questions and was the source of all the important information for our little village. Someone who was going to Cardston and had room for an extra passenger in the car would call Operator and leave word. On the other hand, anyone who needed a ride to Cardston and did not have a way would also call Operator. She was the source of all the information that kept our town connected. On some occasions, information flowed so freely there were more connections than you might want. But that's the way with a small town, and we wouldn't have changed it.

The twentieth century has brought with it unbelievable technology, providing communication through the most sophisticated procedures. It has been described as a period of time that has taken us from "muttering machines to laser beams." With all of the advancement that has been made for many, however, the communication lines remain down with no connection. Not across the ocean or the continent, but across the room, across the table, in our own homes. There are times for many when no one calls and no one answers; and if they do, it is like foreigners at Heathrow Airport — a shrug of the shoulders meaning, "I don't understand you. It doesn't make sense to me. I can hear you, but your message is not getting through."

Some time ago, a young woman traveling from one distant state to another stopped in Salt Lake City. She was en route to her grandmother's home, where she was planning to live for a while. I met her when she visited my office, having called in advance for an appointment. She was an attractive young woman about sixteen years of age. We sat together on the couch in my office, and through the west window, we could see the Salt Lake Temple. She was obviously nervous. At first she responded only to my questions, as I attempted to become acquainted with her. Getting nowhere at all, I finally asked Jennifer (not her real name), "How are things with you at home? Tell me about your family, your brothers and sisters, your parents."

There was silence. She fidgeted with something in her hands, then shook her head and whispered, "It's not good, not good at all." I waited for her to explain further. "You see," she said, tears filling her eyes, "my mom won't ever talk to me, and she won't listen." Biting her lower lip to control her tears, she continued, "She listens to others but not to me. I'm the youngest one in our family, and my mom won't ever listen to me."

"That must be hard," I responded quietly.

"Yes," she said, "because I love my mom. Why won't she talk to me?" she sobbed. "I'm going to live with my grandmother for a while because Mom and I just can't get along."

"Don't get along?"

"Yes, we don't ever talk to each other. It's so hard . . . because"—she hesitated and wiped her eyes—"because I love her."

"Have you ever told her so?" I asked. She shook her head. "Do you think she would like to know? Could you write your feelings and express your love for her in a letter?"

"Maybe."

"Will you?" I asked. She agreed she would. "Would you like to get a letter of love from your mom? And if you did, would you bother to read it?" I asked.

"Yes, oh yes," she whispered.

"And would you answer?"

She nodded.

After listening to Jennifer for some time and allowing her to discuss her concerns, I asked if it would be acceptable with her if I were to call her mother and tell her that we had talked and that she had expressed love for her mother. Without hesitation she agreed, and she gave me the area code and the telephone number for her parents' home.

As Jennifer left my office, I gave her a warm hug and expressed my love. "Thanks, thanks for listening," she said. "I'll write to my mom."

I watched her as she waited at the elevator. The doors opened and she got in and waved good-bye. Then the doors closed and she was gone. Returning to my desk, I asked over and over in my mind, What kind of a mother must this beautiful and sensitive young woman have? I would find out. I dialed the number she had given me.

"Hello," a cheery voice answered. I identified myself and then verified that I was speaking to Jennifer's mother. She certainly sounded pleasant enough, although a bit surprised that I would be calling her.

"I'm calling," I explained, "to tell you of my visit with your daughter."

"Really?"

"I've enjoyed visiting with your daughter. I'm impressed with her," I said. "She tells me she is going to live with her grandmother."

"Yes," her mother responded. "It seems like it might be better that way. But it's very hard." Her voice filled with emotion. "You see, Sister Kapp, the problem is, Jenny won't ever talk to me, and she just won't listen. We can't communicate." Like an echo from a familiar phrase, I heard again, "She won't talk to me, and she won't listen." The woman hesitated, then explained, "I love her so much, but a barrier, like a wall, has grown up between us, and it seems like I can't get through to her."

We talked for some time. I told her of the love her daughter had expressed for her. "I think she would like to get a letter from you," I said, "and maybe you could write about your tender feelings for her."

"I will. I will today," she promised.

Many times since that conversation the familiar phrase plays on the memory of my mind, "She won't talk to me, and she won't listen." I hear the hurt in Jennifer's voice and the anxiety in her mother's. The lines were down. There was no operator to help get the message through, and the distance between them was increasing.

We are all away from home in the sense that we cannot talk to our Father in heaven face to face, and we long to call home, but many times it seems that we can't get through. The fact is that a veil separates us from our heavenly home for a time, but that need never ever keep us from communicating, talking, listening, being in touch, expressing love, and feeling the love our Father has for us. There are times when we may feel far away from home and out of touch, when we've missed our plane connection, so to speak, and the lines are temporarily down. We begin to yearn for that close contact with home, yet feel so far away. We may think, *My Father doesn't talk to me and he doesn't listen. My prayers don't get through.*

And what of the times when we struggle up steep and rocky slopes in times of trials and tests? Is it possible our Father watches tenderly and is willing and anxious to give help and comfort, guidance and warnings, but he can't get through to us because we don't talk to him, and we don't listen even though we have been warned?

"Behold, verily, verily, I say unto you, ye must watch and pray always lest ye enter into temptation; for Satan desireth to have you, that he may sift you as wheat," Jesus taught the Nephites. "Therefore ye must always pray unto the Father in my name." (3 Nephi 18:18–19.)

Too often we fail to ask and we do not listen with full anticipation of receiving an answer. Maybe we really don't even expect an answer.

For some time I have had a little sign on my file cabinet at home that was given to me at a Young Women conference. It says simply, "Remember, you are a child of God. Call home." I've often pondered that simple admonition. What does it mean to call home? Would I use number three as I did as a child, or the international number of twelve digits that I used in the air-port? Is there an area code that must precede the number for me to get through in prayer? And is there a charge? Would I get a bill, and how much might it be? How long could I talk?

Nephi understood how to talk and listen to the Lord. He explained, "I . . . did go into the mount oft, and I did pray oft unto the Lord; wherefore the Lord showed unto me great things." (1 Nephi 18:3.)

First we must desire to talk to our Heavenly Father and to listen to him, knowing that he in turn will talk to us in our minds and in our hearts (D&C 8:2) and will listen to us. There is no question about his promise to us. He has said, "Draw near unto me and I will draw near unto you; seek me diligently and ye shall find me; ask, and ye shall receive; knock, and it shall be opened unto you. Whatsoever ye ask the Father in my name it shall be given unto you, that is expedient for you." (D&C 88:63–64.)

In time and when our hearts are full and we know not that for which we should pray, the Spirit will make intercession for us even without the words. (See Romans 8:26.) Our feelings, our desires are heard through our prayers.

"If ye would hearken unto the Spirit which teacheth a man to pray ye would know that ye must pray; for the evil spirit teacheth not a man to pray, but teacheth him that he must not pray. But behold, I say unto you that ye must pray always, and not faint; that ye must not perform any thing unto the Lord save in the first place ye shall pray unto the Father in the name of Christ, that he will consecrate thy performance unto thee, that thy performance may be for the welfare of thy soul." (2 Nephi 32:8–9.)

The scriptures become personal messages to us when we liken them unto ourselves. (1 Nephi 19:23.) Our Savior becomes our advocate and prays to the Father in our behalf, even pleading our cause. He has said, "Wherefore, Father, spare these my brethren [and we can put our own name here] that believe on my name, that they may come unto me and have everlasting life." (D&C 45:5.)

God is our Father. We are his children. We were together in his presence at one time. Jesus, our elder Brother, has made possible an eternal family relationship when we do our part. Think of it! When we understand that relationship, our prayers become natural and instinctive, personal and very real. If we don't remember this relationship between us and our Father, we experience difficulties with prayer. They become routine and mechanical.

In the Bible Dictionary we read: "Prayer is the act by which the will of the Father and the will of the child are brought into correspondence with each other. The object of prayer is not to change the will of God, but to secure for ourselves and for others blessings that God is already willing to grant, but that are made conditional on our asking for them. Blessings require some work or effort on our part before we can obtain them. Prayer is a form of work, and is an appointed means for obtaining the highest of all blessings." (LDS Edition of the King James Version, 1979, pp. 752–53 of Appendix.)

This form of work requires some important preparation on our part if it is to be effective. In a talk to Church Education teachers in 1956, President Harold B. Lee, who was then a member of the Council of the Twelve, talked about a lesson he had learned from President David O. McKay: "The President made the statement that . . . when we are relaxed in a private room, we are more susceptible [to the promptings of the Spirit]; and that so far as he is concerned, his best thoughts come after he gets up in the morning and is relaxed and thinking about the duties of the day; that impressions come more clearly, as if it were a voice." Then President Lee commented, "Those impressions are right. If we are worried about something and upset in our feelings, the inspiration does not come. If we so live that our minds are free from worry and our conscience is clear and our feelings are right toward one another, the operation of the Spirit of the Lord upon our spirit is as real as when we pick up the telephone; but when they come, we must be brave enough to take the suggested actions." (Talk to seminary and institute of religion teachers, July 6, 1956.)

We learn to talk and we learn to listen, and often while reading the scriptures, we will hear the voice of the Lord in our mind and in our heart by the promptings of the Holy Ghost. (D&C 8:2.) We come to know the Lord's will concerning us as we ponder the direction given in our patriarchal blessings when he speaks to us in a very personal way through his appointed servant, the patriarch.

You will remember the story of Hannah, who prayed for a son and vowed to give him to the Lord. Then Samuel was born, and as a youth he went to live with Eli the priest. One night he had a very personal experience. The Lord called him, and the young boy, thinking it was Eli, ran to Eli and responded, "Here am I. Did you call me?"

Eli explained that he had not called him and counseled the child to lie down again and go back to sleep. The Lord called again. Samuel arose and went to Eli and repeated, "Here am I." Eli responded, "I called not, my son; lie down again."

The Lord called a third time, and Samuel once again said, "Here am I, for thou didst call me." This time Eli perceived that the Lord had called the child, and he counseled him that if he were called again, he was to say, "Speak, Lord; for thy servant heareth."

Once again the Lord called, "Samuel, Samuel." This time Samuel answered, "Speak; for thy servant heareth." (1 Samuel 3:1–10.)

Our Father talks to us as surely as he spoke to Samuel, although perhaps not in the same way, and he listens. We can talk to him and we can listen. When we do, we are never far from home. Our call home allows us to talk as long as we want and to listen as long as we will. The price we pay is simply to always remember him and keep his commandments so that we can have his Spirit with us always.

CHAPTER 15

Of Infinite Worth

I t was early morning, and my thoughts were about young women as I went through some correspondence on my desk. I opened one letter, which began, "Dear Sister Kapp: First of all, let me tell you who I am." I expected a name to follow, but that was not the case. The writer continued, "I am of infinite worth!"

Infinite worth. Oh, how I wish that each young woman could feel that confidence, that assurance, that eternal truth. If only that knowledge could be firmly established in her heart and mind, and she would have the assurance that she, too, is precious in the sight of God, what a great blessing that would be.

Yes, I thought as I read the letter, you are of infinite worth, and so is every other young woman I know and all the ones I don't know. How wonderful it is to know that each one has her own divine mission, a mission that is significant in God's eternal plan. This knowledge can give us peace and purpose even in troubled times. Unfortunately, however, not everyone believes this great truth, and that is sad indeed.

I like the attitude of Charlie Brown, the comic strip character, even when friends makes disparaging remarks. Once Lucy asked her friend Violet, "Do you really think that Charlie Brown is as hopeless as you make him out to be?" Violet responded, "He's worse! He has no redeeming features whatsoever!" And Lucy agreed. "I just can't think of enough bad things to say about him," she said. But Charlie Brown knew better. He stood tall, even against their insults, and made a profound statement: "I'm infinite!" I say, good for Charlie Brown and for everyone else who has come to recognize this great truth.

Often in my travels people will recognize me and comment, "You're Sister Kapp, aren't you?" And I will reply, "Yes, I am." Then, with sincere interest, I will ask, "And who are you?" Too often the answer is, "Oh, I'm nobody." Right then I feel an intense desire to correct the error, to recall the thought, and to introduce the speaker to his or her own magnificent self.

How I wish I could visit with each person individually. First I would listen and then we would talk. I would learn from you and you would learn from me. We would share our thoughts and feelings about important things. I would want you to know that it doesn't matter who we *aren't* when we know who we *are*.

To know who we are is essential to our feelings of self-worth. Within every human soul is a natural longing, bone-marrow deep, to know this. On one occasion when I was visiting the Gilbert family in Arizona, I was invited to join in family prayer. Six-year-old Emily was asked by her father to offer the prayer. After expressing gratitude and asking for blessings for family members, especially her mother, who had an important speaking assignment, Emily closed with these words: "Help us always to remember that we are Gilberts." Then she added, "and to know what that means."

To know who we are and what that means gives a sense of destiny, a feeling of belonging, a tie to an eternal family forever.

Some young people I know are concerned about their heritage because they are aware their parents aren't yet perfect, and they allow feelings of uncertainty about their heritage to creep into their minds. Such concern is shortsighted and foolish. None of us is perfect yet. Our identity extends far beyond this immediate generation and links us to a divine inheritance in which we are to become joint-heirs with Jesus Christ. We lived with him before this earth life, and we will, if we choose to follow him, live with him again in a glorious family relationship.

If we don't know where we came from, it is impossible for

us to know where we are to go. And without this knowledge, we are left to drift along, unable to decide what to do and what not to do, where to go and where not to go. The risk of making wrong decisions is magnified a hundredfold. To consider this life only is like viewing just the second act of a three-act play. If we didn't know what preceded this life or what will follow, nothing would make much sense and nothing would really matter.

One day in the early spring, my little niece Shelly and I walked for hours, carefully picking our way from one rock to the next along the creek bed behind our house. Before long we were drawn to an open field, where we noticed tender green shoots forcing their way through the earthy floor, and the winter snow receding toward the mountain peaks. It seemed as though all of nature bore evidence of God's creations and his great love for us. At the close of this memorable day, we knelt together while she expressed thanks for the creek, the slippery rocks, the meadow, and me. I then gently tucked the covers around her and bent down for a goodnight kiss. Reaching up with both arms around my neck and pulling me close, Shelly whispered, "I wish we were in the same family."

"Shelly, my dear," I quickly explained, "we *are* in the same family."

"I mean the very same family. My last name is Larsen and your last name is Kapp, and that isn't the same. I mean, I wish you were my sister and we had the very same last name."

"Shelly, we really are in the very same family," I replied. "You see, we are all Heavenly Father's children, every one of us. That makes us members of one great family. We are brothers and sisters, and Jesus is our brother too, our Elder Brother."

"Then what is Jesus' last name?" she asked.

"We know our Savior as Jesus the Christ," I said.

With the pure innocence of youth, she began to make us all one family and to secure this relationship by linking my first name with the surname "the Christ."

"Oh no, my dear, we don't put our names together like that," I said.

"Why not?" she asked.

Wanting her to be aware of the sacredness of our relationship with the Savior, I tried to explain. "Maybe it's because sometimes we are not good enough. I don't feel worthy yet."

Suddenly she raised up on her elbow. "What do you do that's wrong? Why don't you stop doing it, and then we can all be in the same family? We can all use his name."

As I pondered the answer to her question, in my mind I heard, as though for the first time, words that I had heard often before, but now it seemed as though I was hearing them with my whole heart and soul: "That they are willing to take upon them the name of thy Son, and always remember him and keep his commandments which he has given them." (D&C 20:77.)

I realized more fully the reality of our relationship with our Elder Brother, Jesus Christ, and a new thought came into my mind. *Not only is he my brother, but I am his sister.* Imagine such a family relationship! All members of the same family—his family. Could we possibly want more?

When I hear people make comments of self-depreciation, I want to open the Book of Mormon and read the words of King Benjamin:

"And now, because of the covenant which ye have made ye shall be called the children of Christ, his sons, and his daughters; for behold, this day he hath spiritually begotten you; for ye say that your hearts are changed through faith on his name; therefore, ye are born of him and have become his sons and his daughters.

"And under this head ye are made free, and there is no other head whereby ye can be made free. There is no other name given whereby salvation cometh; therefore, I would that ye should take upon you the name of Christ, all you that have entered into the covenant with God that ye should be obedient unto the end of your lives. . . .

"Therefore, I would that ye should be steadfast and immovable, always abounding in good works, that Christ, the Lord God Omnipotent, may seal you his, that you may be brought to heaven, that ye may have everlasting salvation and eternal life, through the wisdom, and power, and justice, and mercy of him who created all things, in heaven and in earth, who is God above all." (Mosiah 5:7–8, 15.)

In times of discouragement and self-doubt, we must try to remember who we are, or better, *whose* we are; and when we make a mistake, we must never give up on ourselves. When we hear a beautiful violin that is out of tune, we wouldn't throw the violin away. It has not lost its value. It just needs to be tuned by tightening a string.

And so it is as we make adjustments in our lives through daily repentance and commitment to strive each day to keep the commandments. This is best done through daily prayer, when we ask our Father in heaven what we should do or stop doing to become a better daughter, sister, or friend. And in answer to our questions, as we ponder and listen, thoughts will come into our minds that will guide us. It is that simple. This daily source of strength makes the steep and steady climb upward in this life one of adventure and hope, not of despair and discouragement. Because of the link in our pedigrees, our nature is divine and we have unlimited possibilities. We are of a noble birthright. We are of the royal house of Israel, the chosen ones.

Like a mighty chain of infinite worth, our reach extends in both directions to include all that we have inherited from the past and all that we will yet bring to the future. It is the incredible excitement of this linking of past and future that is enticing many women to become involved in searching out their ancestors through the name-extraction program. As they search the records to find their relatives, marvelous miracles are unfolding. As they find their forefathers, they discover themselves and all those relatives who have preceded them and who continue to care about them.

On one occasion, President Benson said, "The heavenly grandstands are cheering you on." I am convinced that our ancestors care about us and cheer us on. It is important for us to know of our divine nature and our infinite worth.

To know who we are is important, but to know where we are headed is essential if we are to receive all the blessings our Father in heaven has for those who love him and keep his commandments. Our eternal home is our ultimate destination, and we know the way.

One summer at a Young Women conference in Alberta, Canada, three hundred girls were camped in tents scattered among tall pines. It rained every day and was very cold and wet. Even so, there was no murmuring in the camp. The last day of the conference I addressed the young women under cloudy skies. Despite the unseasonable cold, there was a feeling of warmth among them. Maybe because of the cold, we were all drawn together and felt warm from the inside out.

I began my remarks by asking, "Where are you going following this conference?" The united chorus of three hundred young women resounded through the tall pines. "Home!" they cried out. "Where?" I asked again, and they responded with even greater conviction, "Home!" I was convinced they were not interested in any detours. They knew where they were headed and were anxious to get there.

It is essential to our happiness to know not only who we are but also where we are headed. When we know where we are going, the risk of detours because of temporary pleasures, appealing enticements, and alluring voices becomes much less of a threat to our happiness here and in the eternities.

A few years ago, after three weeks away in a faraway country and feeling homesick and lonely, I lay in my bed in a strange hotel and began thinking about home and family. I pictured myself walking up the sidewalk. I could see in my mind's eye the front door of my home. I began to feel the warmth and even the smell of our house. I imagined I felt the warm hugs of family members as they welcomed me back. My mind stretched even further, and I reached to think how it will be when I see again my mother and father. I could almost feel what it will be like when we run, with arms outstretched, into each others' arms and rejoice together and remember happy times. And then I tried to comprehend how it will be to feel the embrace once again of our Father in heaven and of our Elder Brother, and to be safely home forever.

As Latter-day Saints, we know who we are and where we are headed, but many often ask another question: "Why am I here?" That also is important to know. We are here so that we can be tried and tested and so that we can learn right from wrong. We are here with freedom to choose. While there is opposition in all things, we must learn to choose good over evil and be obedient to the laws given by our Father in heaven to help us follow the way. When we left our heavenly home, we knew Satan would be here on earth and would try in every way possible to tempt us, just as he did there. Though his plan was enticing, we chose to come to earth and to follow Jesus Christ and keep his commandments. We knew it would be difficult, that the test would not be easy—but we understood the gospel plan, and we shouted for joy as we anticipated this earthly journey.

Needed today as never before are women who will take a stand for righteousness and resist once again the enticings of the adversary. As we live the laws of the gospel, the powers of Satan are bound among us. Every soul is stronger than Satan if that soul is determined to be obedient and follow the Savior. The Lord has promised us that we will never be tested beyond our ability to withstand.

When we were baptized, we covenanted with, or promised, our Father in heaven that we would serve him and keep his commandments. He in turn covenanted with each of us that he would always be with us and never leave us. Even in times of loneliness or when we may feel worthless, we are not alone and we are not worthless. We did not come to this earth life to gain our worth. We brought it with us. Our responsibility is to grow from our experiences so that we might be prepared for greater responsibilities and opportunities along the way.

As we learn to make and keep sacred covenants, we begin

our preparation to one day have the glorious experience of entering the holy temple of the Lord. There we can receive additional ordinances and covenants, promises, and blessings, providing us with information that is essential to our returning home to the presence of our Father in heaven. In no other place is this great blessing, this gift, this endowment made possible. This magnificent blessing of such eternal significance is within our reach. But for each of us, it requires reaching and stretching and extending ourselves to be more than we are now, but not more than we have the capacity to become. It was never intended that the test would be easy.

I remember a very difficult time in my life when I was having serious problems at school because I had been ill and had missed some basic lessons. School was hard, but worse than that was a feeling of being dumb and unaccepted by my friends. That really hurt. Then my father told me about the temple. He promised me that if I did my very best, learned to be obedient, and continued to be obedient, I could receive a temple recommend, which would verify I was worthy to enter through those doors— to enter that sacred place where I would learn all I needed to know to get back home safely.

I had walked around the temple many times, but that day I set a goal to qualify to go inside. I did not want to remain on the outside. I wanted to go inside. It is inside the temple that we can receive ordinances and covenants that will eventually admit us, if we remain worthy, into the presence of our Father in heaven, with the anticipation of a glorious homecoming. It was then that I began to realize the purpose of this life and that the greatest of all blessings, the blessing of exaltation, was within my reach. It is within the reach of all who strive to live worthily and keep the commandments.

As each new day begins, as sure as the sun comes up and the sun goes down, there will be ups and downs in our lives, not to make us sad, but to provide opportunities for growth that will make us glad. This is a wonderful world and a most remarkable time to live. The gospel has been restored to the earth in its fulness. As President Ezra Taft Benson has said, pointing to the special mission of this generation, "While our generation will be comparable in wickedness to the days of Noah, when the Lord cleansed the earth by flood, there is a major difference this time: God has saved for the final inning some of His stronger and most valiant children, who will help bear off the kingdom triumphantly. . . . You are the generation that must be prepared to meet your God." (*Ensign,* April 1987, p. 73.)

In view of this challenging time for which we have been reserved, we can expect some pain, discouragement, disappointments, trials, and temptations. When we choose to follow the Savior, we can expect some suffering, some loneliness, and some injustice. But in times such as this, it is well to remember the words of Elder Orson F. Whitney: "No pain that we suffer, no trial that we experience is wasted. It ministers to our education, to the development of such qualities as patience, faith, fortitude, and humility. All that we suffer and all we endure, especially when we endure it patiently, builds up our character, purifies our heart, expands our souls, and makes us more tender and charitable, more worthy to be called the children of God. It is through sorrow and suffering, toil and tribulation that we gain the education that we came here to acquire and which will make us more like our Father and Mother in Heaven."

The challenges we face are real. We will always face tests. They may take the form of peer pressure – the need to feel that we belong, the pressure to follow the crowd. They may include hungering for popularity, beauty, money, position, clothes, and other outward symbols that supposedly say, "Look at me. I am really somebody. I am accepted." And yet one can have all these things and still feel empty inside. It is at such times that we need to remember who we are and where we are headed. It is then that we need self-discipline and strength to avoid the detours that offer only momentary pleasure and too often leave lasting scars.

Every day and in every way, Satan uses every possible means to have us within his grasp. Sometimes his tactics call for subtle –

or even not so subtle—messages in entertainment, music, and videos. Sometimes his enticements involve disobedience, dishonesty, distrust, or contention, or they may take the form of immodesty, immorality, or vulgarity. If we have a weakness, it may be at that very spot that we are tested the most. When people lack integrity—if their actions do not fit their beliefs—great destruction takes place inside them. It begins slowly. First they don't like themselves, resulting in loss of respect, self-esteem, and faith. Then they begin to dislike others, and contention crowds in. And soon, as a result of such insidious forces, the Spirit is forced to leave.

Obedience to God's commandments, which are provided only for our safety and welfare, brings feelings of self-mastery, self-confidence, self-worth, and increased faith. When we know we are striving to do God's will, our attitude can change from "I can't" to a feeling that "with God's help, I can."

Setting righteous goals and then reaching and stretching to attain them is a process that develops our ability to be in control of ourselves. It helps us to overcome temptation and develop the power to resist anger, hatred, jealousy, envy. We can overcome feelings of inferiority, inadequacy, and incompetence.

This life is not intended to be easy. But safety and protection are within our reach as we choose to be obedient to God's plan. He loves us and he wants us to return home, but he will not force us. We have to do our part too. If we have faith and pray humbly, he will encourage, strengthen, guide, and direct us, through the whisperings of the Holy Ghost. We can also turn to the scriptures, which are like letters from home—messages from our Father and his servants, the prophets, to comfort us, guide us, warn us, and teach us of his magnificent, unwavering love for us.

In the Book of Mormon, we read of the wise counsel Helaman gave to his sons. The counsel is equally good for daughters: "Remember, remember that it is upon the rock of our Redeemer, who is Christ, the Son of God, that ye must build your foundation; that when the devil shall send forth his mighty winds, yea, his shafts in the whirlwind, yea, when all his hail and his mighty storm shall beat upon you, it shall have no power over you to drag you down to the gulf of misery and endless wo, because of the rock upon which ye are built, which is a sure foundation, a foundation whereon if men build they cannot fall." (Helaman 5:12.)

There is no limit to our greatness, our wonderful uniqueness. Each of us is of infinite worth, and each of us has much to share. It isn't intended that we should all progress in the same way at the same speed. Someone has said, "Anyone who imagines that all fruits ripen at the same time as the strawberries knows nothing about grapes."

Our Father has told us that he will try our patience and our faith. (See Mosiah 23:21.) It is in our daily prayers, as we ask for specific help, that our burdens are eased and we are given strength to endure all things. Here are excerpts from letters of some young women who have made this discovery in their lives:

"For the past nine months I didn't go to church. I was going through a real difficult time, and I just ran away from it. Then I was asked to sing in the girls' chorus. I am so thankful that I accepted this invitation. The Spirit was so strong that I just cried. I now realize that I need the gospel in my life. I realize that Heavenly Father loves me very much. I have a strong testimony of the gospel, and I love it with all my heart."

"My family and I have gone through a lot this year, for my parents got a divorce. I have been calling this my wilderness time. One night as I was reading my scriptures, I came to Alma, chapter 34, verse 26. Many times I had known I needed to pray, but I didn't feel worthy. This scripture was just what I needed. It is during the hard times that the Lord can help us most. I could never make it alone."

"You might have called me a lost sheep. My behavior did not show the royal birthright that I had partaken of just a short time ago. My grades showed lack of interest; my language, a lack of caring. Then I got a new adviser in the Young Women program who treated me as a daughter of God. Pretty soon I

The Joy of the Journey

found myself excited about the gospel. I found that my testimony, which had atrophied to the size of a needle point, was growing. I found my love for the Savior and his love for me increasing and bonding into one eternal friendship. I found that my self-esteem, which had been at a drastically low rate, was rising. And I found the one thing I needed most—friends. The Young Women program was full of them. I also found that the best Friend I could ever have is only a prayer away. I have been a Latter-day Saint all my life, but I have never been so excited about the gospel as I am now. I know that the Lord blesses us continually and helps us find the things we need to get back home."

"The Spirit gives me strength to keep plowing right through all the trials that Satan puts in my way. My patriarchal blessing tells me that the adversary shall have no power over me because of my testimony and obedience. I know I can be strong. My heart is so full, and there is so much I want to say. This joy is more than any joy that new clothes bring. This joy is uplifting. It fills my whole being with happiness in a time in my life when I need it the most.

"I love this gospel, and I will strive to live the commandments of God all my life. I know that I am a daughter of a Heavenly Father who loves me, and I love him. I hope that I can always be an example to others and that they might be touched by my strong testimony of the gospel. I hope that I can find the lost sheep of the Lord's flock. I will stand for truth and righteousness and hold my torch high for everyone to see that I love the Lord and his gospel."

Yes, the young women of the Church are youth of a noble birthright. They are of infinite worth. Oh, how I yearn for every one of them to know and feel the strength that comes from knowing who she is, where she is headed, and the purpose of this earth life! When we understand the reason for the tests and even the suffering, and especially when we know that our Savior knows us and has felt every pang of suffering that has ever been felt by anyone at any time, our struggle can become easier.

We learn in the Book of Mormon that Jesus Christ himself suffered "pains and afflictions and temptations of every kind; and this that the word might be fulfilled which saith he will take upon him the pains and the sicknesses of his people; . . . and he will take upon him their infirmities, that his bowels may be filled with mercy, according to the flesh, that he may know according to the flesh how to succor his people according to their infirmities." (Alma 7:11–12.)

No, we cannot tell him anything about disappointments or heartaches, loneliness or rejection, pain or heartbreak. He knows and understands it all. He suffered and died for each one of us. He also knows and understands us and stands ready to comfort us at all times. He is our Brother, our Lord and Savior, and his Father is our Father. We have inherited his divine qualities, even to become perfect as he is, although not in this lifetime. Yet at some future time, with his help, even this goal is within our reach. We are of infinite worth with infinite possibilities when we know who we are and what that means. As we learn to accept ourselves, even as we are striving for improvement, marvelous blessings open up and enormous opportunities await us.

It is often while we are facing challenges that we discover our strengths and experience deep feelings of accomplishments. I hope every woman, young and older, will come to know about the steep climbs to the mountain peaks and also the great lessons to be learned in the valleys. I am glad God allows us to struggle, to cry, and to feel pain. I am glad we know about hurt and healing, about fear and faith, about offenses and forgiveness, about discouragement and encouragement. I am grateful to know about the grace of God and his infinite love.

I know, from personal experience, that when we do our very best and give our total effort, the Lord will do the rest in matters that affect safe travel toward eternal life and exaltation. And while we travel homeward, there will be those along the way to whom we can reach out with encouragement, friendship, service, example, and righteous influence, for each person we meet is truly of infinite worth.

CHAPTER 16

Someone Will Know

I have a drawing of the Tower of Pisa that I have kept over the years because of the message it conveys. The encyclopedia refers to this structure as the Leaning Tower of Pisa, and having been to Italy and seen it, I think there is no question that description is correct. However, the drawing I have presents the tower in absolutely perpendicular form, straight up and down, no tilt whatsoever. It towers 184.5 feet into the air. The marble walls that were once white are thirteen feet thick at the base. History records that early on, the foundation for the structure began to give way, and by the mid-twentieth century the tower was leaning more than seventeen feet. Today it continues to slip and is threatened with collapse.

My cartoon illustration of the tower includes two architects standing in front of it with blueprints in hand, obviously satisfied with their magnificent accomplishment, and one tells the other, "We skimped a little on the foundation, but no one will ever know."

Recently that cartoon came to mind again, and I thought about the consequences of faulty foundations. As I was driving my thirteen-year-old nephew Kent to a piano recital, a new billboard loomed before us on the highway. A picture of two large skis, polished and enticing, filled one-half of the sign. The other half, in bold letters, read, "Take two and call in sick." It might have added, "No one will ever know."

"What do you think about that sign?" I asked Kent.

His answer came quickly. "I'm going to own my own business when I grow up. I'll be my own boss. I won't have to ask."

"But if you weren't the boss and wanted to go skiing, then what?" A long discussion began.

What does it really mean to be honest? Someone has said, "When you begin to tell little white lies that seem harmless at first, you soon become color blind." Honesty is like the foundation of character. The foundation must be sound if the building is to stand erect. Our strength of character, our reputation, our trustworthiness, and ultimately our peace of mind rest heavily on the foundation of honesty.

We know that Satan, having rebelled against God, became the father of all lies. (See Moses 4:4.) Deception, cheating, fraud, dishonesty, and even deliberate misrepresentation are all tactics found in his bag of tools with the intent to destroy us. His tactics are subtle. He would have us begin by rationalizing, slipping just a little. Surely just a little indiscretion can't be too serious, especially if no one would ever know. It's just a marginal lie. He says, "Eat, drink, and be merry; nevertheless, fear God—he will justify [us] in committing a little sin; yea, lie a little, take the advantage of one because of his words, dig a pit for thy neighbor; there is no harm in this; and do all these things, for tomorrow we die." (2 Nephi 28:8.)

The Lord in his mercy and love provides warnings, commandments, laws, and standards to protect us. He warns, "Behold, verily, verily, I say unto you, ye must watch and pray always lest ye enter into temptation; for Satan desireth to have you, that he may sift you as wheat." (3 Nephi 18:18.) When a foundation begins to slip, if it is not corrected there is a serious threat of collapse, a falling down.

Lying weakens our faith; it weakens confidence. Mark Twain knew about this process. His Huckleberry Finn described how it works: "I about made up my mind to pray, and see if I couldn't try to quit bein' the kind of a boy I was and be better. So I kneeled down. But the words wouldn't come. Why wouldn't they? It warn't no use to try and hide it from Him. . . . I knowed very

When the bell rang and I walked away, now misty-eyed, from this group of boys, I was thinking: "Bobby, little brown skin, with your clear, bright, dark eyes and your straight, trim, lithe body—Bobby, at 14 you are a better man than I. Thank you for climbing so very, very high today." (Elam Hill, "A Boy and A Rope," *Teacher's Journal*.)

Under such pressure, some might have wondered what difference does it really make, and said, "No one will ever know." The truth is, Bobby would know and God would know, and that is a majority.

We will each be tried and tested during our lifetime to see if we will keep the commandments of God and walk uprightly before him. Consider what Bobby Polacio learned about himself at the moment he made his decision to report the truth. Compare his feelings with what they would have been had he chosen to rationalize, justify, and deceive. What do we learn about ourselves when the pressure is on?

Erma Bombeck, in her newspaper column, discussed cheating and asked what kind of messages we are sending with the following mentality: "You can't break into a car, but it's OK to fish without a license. You can't steal a bicycle, but it's all right to filch a few office supplies. Don't lie to your mother, but you can tell the person at the box office you're big for 11." (*Deseret News*, January 31, 1992.)

As Latter-day Saints, we covenant to keep the commandments, not only for the reason of obedience, but also for our own blessing and benefit. We covenant to keep the commandments so that we can have the Spirit of the Lord with us. Lying, stealing, shoplifting, cheating, disobeying the laws of God— these all damage a person's spirit. When we go contrary to what we know to be right, we become less receptive to the promptings of the Holy Ghost. Lying affects not only our spiritual well-being but also our physical bodies, and we pay a severe price for such behavior. Lewis Thomas, through the eyes of science, had this to say:

As I understand it, a human being cannot tell a lie, even a small one, without setting off a kind of smoke alarm somewhere deep in a dark lobule of the brain, resulting in the sudden discharge of nerve impulses, or the sudden outpouring of neurohormones of some sort, or both. The outcome, recorded by the lie-detector gadgetry, is a highly reproducible cascade of changes in the electrical conductivity of the skin, the heart rate, and the manner of breathing, similar to the responses to various kinds of stress.

Lying, then, is stressful, even when we do it for protection, or relief, or escape, or profit, or just for the pure pleasure of lying and getting away with it. It is a strain, distressing enough to cause the emission of signals to and from the central nervous system warning that something has gone wrong. It is, in a pure physiological sense, an unnatural act. (*Late Night Thoughts on Listening to Mahler's Ninth Symphony*, New York: Bantam Books, 1984, p. 128.)

On Wednesday, May 22, 1974, the *Salt Lake Tribune* carried an article about Jeb Stewart Magruder, who had been sentenced to serve in a federal prison for his part in the Watergate scandal in Washington, D.C. Magruder was quoted as saying, "It has been nearly impossible for me to face the disappointment I see in the eyes of my friends, the confusion I see in the eyes of my children, the heartbreak I see in the eyes of my wife, and probably more difficult the contempt I see in the eyes of others. My ambition obscured my judgment. By now I know what I have done and your honor knows what I have done," Magruder told the judge. "Somewhere between my ambition and my ideals I lost my ethical compass."

Our ethical compass comes from our conscience, our knowledge of what we know to be right. A few months ago I received a letter from a young man that reads in part: "This letter comes to you from within the walls of the Utah State Prison. Whether or not you listen is your choice—but I want you to know that what I will say comes from my heart. I write this because I don't want to see you make the same mistakes that I've made, and I testify before God that what I will say is the truth. It could be that only one basic decision is all that will separate you from someday joining me here in prison. That decision is whether or not you will choose to follow God. Please don't underestimate how critically important this choice is, for in the long run it is truly the difference between life and death, between heaven and hell, between happiness and misery."

His tragic letter goes on to explain, "I had fun at first. Nearly everyone does. I had heard about the dangers, but I thought I was too strong and smart to have any problems." And so his journey to the state prison began with only a small crack and a minor slip. The fall from integrity does not happen with a minor slip. It comes tumbling down gradually with one small decision after another, acting contrary to your knowledge of right and wrong.

In the book *The Making of George Washington,* we read about a rule that young George Washington learned from his father:

"Labor to keep alive in your breast that little speck of celestial fire called conscience."

"What is conscience, Father?" asked George.

His father explained:

"All of us have standards of right and wrong that we have acquired from various sources. The most important of these sources is the Bible. You have also learned from your mother and from me, many things that you *should,* and some things that you *should not* do. Some standards are quite definite. . . . For example, you know that you must tell the truth, no matter what it may cost you. There are many other laws that are just as clear. The Ten Commandments are quite precise.

"But the exact laws are only a part of our standards. There is another great field of conduct. . . . In all cases . . . your conscience tells you when you are doing wrong. It is both a guide to action, and a check on your past conduct. If we do something wrong . . . or do something that is contrary to God's laws, or the rules of our family, there is something inside us that tells us that we are not living up to those standards. That is conscience." (William H. Wilbur, *The Making of George Washington* DeLand, Florida: Patriotic Education, Inc., 1970, p. 85.)

151

Consider the message in the following essay, titled "Habit," by an unknown writer:

> I am your constant companion. I am your greatest helper or heaviest burden. I will push you onward or drag you down to failure. I am completely at your command. Half the things you do you might just as well turn over to me, and I will be able to do them quickly and correctly.
>
> I am easily managed. You must merely be firm with me. Show me exactly how you want something done and after a few lessons I will do it automatically. I am the servant of all great men; and alas, of all failures as well. Those who are great, I have made great. Those who are failures, I have made failures.
>
> I am not a machine, though I work with all the precision of a machine plus the intelligence of a man. You may run me for profit or run me for ruin—it makes no difference to me.
>
> Take me, train me, be firm with me, and I will place the world at your feet. Be easy with me, and I will destroy you. Who am I? I am habit!

The habit of honesty becomes the foundation of character. Every day we build that foundation by the choices we make, ever so small.

President Lorenzo Snow taught: "The Lord has determined in his heart that he will try us until he knows what he can do with us. He tried his son Jesus thousands of years before he came upon the earth. The Father had watched his course and knew he could depend upon him when the salvation of worlds should be at stake and he was not disappointed. So in regard to ourselves he will try us and continue to try us in order that he may place us in the highest positions in life and put upon us the most sacred responsibilities." (*The Millennial Star*, August 24, 1899, p. 532.)

There are tragic examples of individuals whose character has been destroyed because they thought that no one would ever know about their acts of willful carelessness or dishonesty. And throughout history there are those whose integrity is as inspiring today as it was at the moment it was acted out. One such man was Sir Thomas More, the clergyman who opposed King Henry VIII when the king desired to divorce his wife, Catherine of Aragon, in order to marry Anne Boleyn. The story of this struggle has been dramatized in the play and movie *A Man for All Seasons*. For various reasons, what Henry was asking violated More's conscience, and he would not sign an oath in support of the king. As a result, he gradually lost everything: his station, his position, his wealth, even his physical comforts, for he was imprisoned in the Tower of London. His captors used every means to tempt him and try to induce him to give in and sign the oath to the king. He wouldn't do it. He maintained silence.

Then More's daughter came to him and pleaded, "Oh, Father, do you know what it is like at home without you? We can't even afford candles there. It is a miserable life. You've taught me all my life that God regards the heart, not the words of the lips. Father, take this oath with your lips, but think otherwise in your heart."

He answered her, "Daughter, what is an oath but words you speak to God!" And, cupping his hands, he continued, "My oath is my life. I hold it in my hands like water. If I ever open my hands, I can never expect to find my life again."

And finally, a familiar yet powerful example of honesty and integrity comes to us from the story of Karl G. Maeser, a former president of Brigham Young University. He told his young friends: "I have been asked what I mean by word of honor. I will tell you. Place me behind prison walls—walls of stone ever so high, ever so thick, reaching ever so far into the ground—there is a possibility that in some way or another I may be able to escape, but stand me on that floor and draw a chalk line around me and have me give my word of honor never to cross it. Can I get out of that circle? I'd rather die first!"

In the booklet *For the Strength of Youth*, the First Presidency writes: "You cannot do wrong and feel right. It is impossible. Be honest with yourself. Be honest with others. Be honest with the Lord." God help us all to do so.

CHAPTER 17

Destroying the
Crickets of Our Day

T his is a glorious time to live, but it is also a very threatening and frightening time, especially if we are not prepared. When we are prepared, there is no need to fear. (D&C 38:30.) We are the pioneers of today and are blazing a trail into a wilderness unlike and perhaps even more challenging than that of the pioneers of earlier days. Our courage must be equal to, if not greater than, that of pioneers like young Mary Goble Pay. From her journal we read:

> We arrived in Salt Lake City 9 o'clock at night, the 9th of December, 1856. Three out of the four who were living were frozen. My mother was dead in the wagon. Early next morning Brigham Young came. When he saw our condition, our feet frozen and our mother dead, tears rolled down his cheeks. The doctor amputated my toes while the sisters were dressing Mother for her grave. When my feet were fixed, they carried us into see our mother for the last time. That afternoon she was buried. I have thought often of my mother's words before we left England. "Polly, I want to go to Zion while my children are small so they can be raised in the gospel of Jesus Christ for I know this is the true church."

Do mothers today care that much for the gospel and for their children? Of course they do. For many, it may seem easier to die in the wagon than to stand guard every day in defending and upholding standards of righteousness. It may seem easier to die for the gospel in an effort to save their children than to live for it. But live it they must, so their children will not die spiritually.

And for many young women, it may seem easier to have their toes amputated than be a pioneer today and stand on their feet in front of their peers and dare to be different if their peers' actions violate what the Holy Spirit whispers is right. We are warned in the scriptures, "Yea, and all that will live godly in Christ Jesus shall suffer persecution." (2 Timothy 3:12.) Peer pressure is a form of persecution. It is one of the great tests of today.

Do you remember the story of the early pioneers and how the terrible plague of black crickets came down from the mountains to destroy the crops of grain? Men, women, and children prayed and fought these ravaging crickets in a desperate effort to save their crops. The Lord heard their earnest prayers and sent sea gulls, which devoured the crickets. The crops were saved. "It is a miracle!" the people said.

Our young women are the tender crops of today, the promise of tomorrow. President Gordon B. Hinckley has taught us that when we save one young woman, we save generations. Every single one counts so very, very much.

In all soberness I ask all women—young women, mothers, leaders—to consider the black crickets of our day that are trying to destroy our tender crops, not only our young women and young men, but many adults also. We have been warned by our prophets that the forces of evil will increase under Lucifer's leadership and the forces of good will increase under the leadership of Jesus Christ. The heat of that great confrontation is becoming more intense. Sooner or later, either privately or publicly, we will all be tested. We must be prepared to defend our values, our standards, our commitment to "stand as witnesses of God at all times and in all things, and in all places." (Mosiah 18:9.)

The crickets of our day are different from those of times past. They are more powerful, more dangerous, and less noticeable. Let me explain. At first things may appear to be very innocent.

Thoughts, words, and pictures are placed into our minds in subtle and sophisticated ways. Thoughts come first and are then expressed through words. No one uses vulgar, crude words without first having thought of them. Can you see how damaging such innocent beginnings are? If we are not watchful, the crickets will creep into our safe places, our homes, our hearts, our minds. Through TV, radio, magazines, movies, literature, music, and fashions, these evil influences will aggressively begin their silent destruction, multiplying their forces as they go.

Many television programs and videos portray immoral behavior as exciting and acceptable ways to express love. Exposure to these messages of deception will dull one's senses until what appeared alarming at first becomes of little concern and even acceptable. If this happens, that falsehood is unmasked. The individual's dreams become nightmares, and hopes are destroyed.

Music has a beautiful and powerful influence in establishing feelings and moods that can lift and elevate our thoughts and our actions. Because it is so powerful, it is cleverly used by the adversary to stimulate thoughts, feelings, and moods, to pollute and poison minds, and to entice individuals to do things they would not otherwise consider.

Each of us wants to be well groomed, to look nice and be attractive. But we must be alert to the aggressive advertising of immodest fashions. Often the desire and practice of wearing such fashions begins innocently and early. Some unwise mothers dress their little girls in ways that unwittingly train their appetite for the immodest fashions of the world, and when they are teenagers, the pattern is set and it is hard to change.

When the counsel of our prophet to avoid dating until sixteen is disregarded, I say that is crickets. Early dating gives Satan a foothold. Single dating at an early age is an invitation for the adversary to attack while young people are away from the safety of the group. Immoral conduct, alcohol, drug abuse, the addicting and degrading effects of pornography, Satan worship, and other cult activities—these are all tools of the adversary and are carefully designed to enslave people and ultimately destroy them. The battle between good and evil is very real. We determine by the choices we make each day where we stand, what our values are, and whom we have chosen to follow.

Melinda, a young pioneer of our day, wrote about how hard it was for her to have the courage to leave her friends when they were seeing a movie that was popular but clearly against her standards. "Some may think, 'It's just a movie, what's the big deal?' " she explained. "But it's the little things that turn into big things. It's not easy to do, but the Lord will help us." When she left the movie, others followed her. That's pioneering.

I am convinced that most young people will respond when they see no faltering, wavering, or weakening on parents' and leaders' part. How older role models live can make a great difference in how their children and other youths live. We must consider carefully our standards and practices, because those who are looking up to us will follow. How will our youth know which way to go if there is no standard that is clearly taught by precept and example?

I firmly believe that activities and practices, even traditions that do not adhere to gospel standards, can be changed. Young people can unite and use positive peer influence to help bring about needed change. There is great power to change when there is unity—in families, wards and stakes, neighborhoods and schools—especially when youth are motivated by righteous principles.

The Lord sent sea gulls to help those early Saints, but sea gulls are not the answer for us today. *Spirituality* is. We live in a world where many voices and influences are attempting to deceive youth and adults. We might honestly wonder, "How can I know for sure? Some things that are so enticing seem so innocent at first." There is a sure way to know. Just as the Lord sent the sea gulls to destroy the crickets, he has provided safety and protection for us. Spirituality allows us to have the Lord's Spirit with us. And when we do, we will not be deceived. He promises us, "I will . . . be your light in the wilderness . . . [if] ye shall keep my commandments." (1 Nephi 17:13.)

When we were baptized and then confirmed as members of The Church of Jesus Christ of Latter-day Saints, each of us was given the gift of the Holy Ghost. The Holy Ghost will help us recognize good and evil, right and wrong, and will teach us and help us remember the lessons we learned even before our earth life. He will strengthen us, comfort us, and give us peace. But there is something important we must never forget. To have the companionship of the Holy Ghost, we must be clean—and to be clean, we must keep the commandments of God. Let me say it another way: When we keep the commandments, we are clean; and when we are clean in our thoughts, our words, and our actions, we can hear the whisperings of the Holy Ghost. In answer to our prayers, we will feel what is right and will be able to discern between good and evil.

Every right choice can conquer a cricket. Rebelling against the laws and standards that God has given to protect us would be like killing the seagulls to preserve the crickets. Standards of the Church have been given to protect us and help us grow spiritually.

When the pioneers ended a day's journey, each night they checked their wagons for any needed repairs. They united in prayer for continued guidance and protection and took a reading of both distance and direction to see how far they had traveled and make sure they were on the right trail. We would do well to follow the same pattern today. A good measurement to ask concerning every important decision is whether this decision will move us toward or away from making and keeping sacred covenants and preparing to receive the ordinances of the temple.

As a sister and friend, I ask you—today and in the days to come, will you think seriously about what it means to be a pioneer today? Talk these things over with your family and friends. Make a firm commitment to be guided by the Spirit concerning what you will do and what you will not do. At nightfall review your actions prayerfully, asking Heavenly

Father for strength to live righteously so that you will hear and feel the whisperings of the Holy Ghost guiding you. Pray for forgiveness in those areas where you have fallen short and ask for strength to do better. When you do this, Father in heaven will hear your prayers, and you will feel added strength and will become a powerful influence for good. A real pioneer!

FOLLOWING
THE PATH

CHAPTER 18

In His Steps

Ohne of the most soul-stretching, soul-refining, yet humbling thoughts for us to contemplate is the possibility that we, with all of our weaknesses and frailties and imperfections, could hope to walk in Jesus' steps, and that he will help us to do so, not just once in a while when we are in deep trouble, but daily, even hourly. This thought has awakened within my heart and soul a sense of our immeasurable possibilities. This point of doctrine from a Latter-day Saint perspective is expressed in a familiar couplet by President Lorenzo Snow: "As man is, God once was; and as God is, man may become."

Those who do not understand this eternal relationship between God and man consider this thought to be blasphemous, sacrilegious, and even nonsense, to say the least. One might ask, "What does it mean to walk in his steps? Surely we can't go all the way." Is it just part of the way, part of the time? Is it just a figure of speech or an intriguing but impossible reality? As Latter-day Saints, we take Jesus' words of invitation to be literal. "Come, follow me, and I will give you rest." "I am the bread of life." "I will feed you." "I am the light in the darkness." "I will guide you." "He who follows me shall never thirst." He promises, "My peace I give unto you." Is it possible that these words have become so familiar that our sensitivity to their profound meaning has become dulled, if not forgotten? The words *rest, bread, water,* and *peace* are household words, yet they become the markers along the path when we choose to follow in his steps and become joint-heirs with him. What an inheritance!

A revelation given through the Prophet Joseph Smith at Kirtland reads: "Verily, thus saith the Lord: It shall come to pass that every soul who forsaketh his sins and cometh unto me, and calleth on my name, and obeyeth my voice, and keepeth my commandments, shall see my face and know that I am." (D&C 93:1.)

With the twentieth century has come an explosion of opportunities for all of us, with ever-expanding vistas and many voices of invitation. But there has also come an invasion of our peace of mind. We wonder how we can do it all. Often there are feelings of confusion and discontent with ourselves. Some of us carry a sense of failure, of falling short of whatever we think we ought to be doing or what we think others think they ought to be doing, given all the options. Even the demands for physical well-being cause us to count calories, fat grams, pounds, and anything else that we can measure and compare.

A friend of mine told of having someone proudly reporting that she'd just finished fifty push-ups that very morning. My friend, dejected by comparison and a few pounds overweight, reported that she couldn't even do five. She felt terrible until the one reporting clarified her success: "I didn't say I did fifty push-ups this morning. I said I finished fifty. I began in 1985."

Someday I'm going to write a book called "The Least Behind That I've Ever Been." Maybe we don't have to catch up before we can rest. The Lord said: "Come unto me, all ye that labour and are heavy laden, and I will give you rest. Take my yoke upon you, and learn of me; for I am meek and lowly in heart: and ye shall find rest unto your souls. For my yoke is easy, and my burden is light." (Matthew 11:28–30.)

If we choose to accept his invitation and follow in his steps, it is essential that we learn who we are and develop a personal identity with our Savior and strive each day to follow him and his example.

A need for a sense of our own identity is, as some say, a

need that is bone-marrow deep. Without having a clear sense of our identity, we become vulnerable to Satan's snares. You will remember that after Jesus had fasted forty days, Satan came to tempt him and tried to place some doubt on his identity, saying, "If thou be the Son of God, command that these stones be made bread." (Matthew 4:3.) Jesus' strength came in knowing who he was—the Son of God. As a young boy, he had said to his mother, "Wist ye not that I must be about my Father's business?" (Luke 2:49), and his last words on the cross were,"Father, into thy hands I commend my spirit" (Luke 23:46). In knowing who he was, he could withstand persecution and abuse. Though he was accused of blasphemy and treason, he felt only love for all, including his enemies. Knowing of his relationship to his Father in heaven, he never wavered. In the hour of greatest agony, he still looked to God, his Father, saying, "Not my will, but thine, be done." (Luke 22:42.)

If we are to walk in his steps, we know our relationship to God, our Father, and to his Son, Jesus Christ. Do we know who we are and, more importantly, *whose* we are?

I have in my file a little poem by Ora Pate Stewart, simple yet profound, about a mother teaching her child. The mother speaks:

> Do you know who you are, little child of mine,
> So precious and dear to me?
> Do you know you're a part of a great design
> That is vast as eternity?
> Can you think for a moment how much depends
> On your holding the "Iron Rod"?
> Your life is forever—worlds without end.
> Do you know you're a child of God?
>
> Do you know where you've been, little child of mine?
> It is hard to recall, I know.
> Do you ever remember that home divine
> With the Father who loves you so?
> Do you sometimes review how He took your hand
> And placed it within my own,

Saying, "Here is a child from Angel Land;
Not a gift, but a precious loan"?

Do you know where you're going, child of mine?
Are your eyes on the road ahead?
Do the spires of His castle gleam and shine
Where the sun grows golden red?
Are you taking enough for your journey, child?
Does your lamp cast a steady glow?
Can you hold your course when the storm is wild?
You will make it, my child, I know.

Knowing who we are will sustain us and strengthen us when the path is steep. The story is told of a young boy who had suffered ridicule and was called names by his peers because of his family background and his questionable parentage. When the boy was twelve years of age a stranger, a preacher, approached him and asked, "Who are you, son? Whose boy are you?" "I felt the old weight of embarrassment come on me," the boy later recalled. But then the preacher looked into his face and began to smile a big smile of recognition. "Wait a minute," he said. "I know who you are. I see the family resemblance. You are a son of God. Boy, you've got a great inheritance. Go claim it."

In later years the boy, now a man, explained, "That was the most important single sentence ever said to me."

President George Q. Cannon years ago stated, "We are the children of God, and as His children there is no attribute we ascribe to Him that we do not possess, though they may be dormant or in embryo. The mission of the Gospel is to develop these powers and make us like our Heavenly Parent." (George Q. Cannon, *Gospel Truth*, Salt Lake City: Deseret Book, 1987, p. 1.)

Our patriarchal blessings identify our lineage, our ancestry. That identification is revealed through an authorized servant of the Lord set apart to be a patriarch. Sometimes we don't understand the significance of this remarkable information in addition to the blessing that goes with it.

When I try to comprehend the Savior's profound, all-encompassing, perfect model, his examples seem to me to fall between two bedrock, secure, immovable pillars that even in our finite way can serve each of us. The first pillar: After he turned the water into wine in Cana, cleansed the temple, taught a woman of Samaria, and healed an invalid on the Sabbath, he faced his accusers and explained: "I seek not mine own will, but the will of the Father which hath sent me." (John 5:30.) The second pillar is his statement given at the close of his mortal life. "Father, the hour is come," he said. Then he gave a report: "I have finished the work which thou gavest me to do." (John 17:4.)

We follow our Savior, not by filling the same mission that he filled, but by seeking to do the will of the Father who has sent us and to do it in such a way that, at the close of our ministry and our mortal life, we might be able to say, as did Jesus, "I have finished the work thou gavest me to do."

President George Q. Cannon explained: "God has chosen us out of the world and has given us a great mission. I do not entertain a doubt myself but that we were selected and fore-ordained for the mission before the world was, that we had our parts allotted to us in this mortal state of existence as our Savior had his assigned to him." (*Gospel Truth*, p. 22.)

It was Mary, the mother of the Savior, who set the pattern for all women, for all times, when she responded to the angel Gabriel, "Behold the handmaid of the Lord; be it unto me according to thy word." (Luke 1:38.)

Have you on occasion, as I have, asked the question, "Father, what is my work, my mission, my purpose?" I remember a difficult time in my life when I pled with the Lord to know what he would have me do, and I learned that you don't receive a witness "until after the trial of your faith." (Ether 12:6.) One dark day years ago when the future seemed bleak and the answer to my prayers seemed, I thought, to be unheard, a little child knocked on my door and asked if my children could come out and play. When I explained to him that I didn't have any children, he put into words what I'd never dared to voice: "Well, if you're not a mother, then what are you?"

In the eternal scheme, according to God's plan, it is most desirable for a woman to be a wife and a mother and a grandmother and the mother of the bride and the mother of a missionary. But some must find fulfillment in other ways: maybe in a scientific laboratory fighting disease, or in a courtroom fighting to defend the laws. Whatever our circumstance, I have come to believe that our mission, our purpose, our work, is to be righteous men and women seeking not our own will but the will of the Father who has sent us. On each point of decision, at every crossroads, let us operate out of a desire to one day report, "Father, I have finished the work which thou gavest me to do."

We each have our own customized crosses to bear, tailored for our individual growth. For some it may be physical, spiritual, or mental illness; for others, poverty and rejection. For some, the test may be to forgive, to repent, and to believe. And most of us in one way or another are weighed down with the heavy cross of pride. We remember President Ezra Taft Benson's warning to us: "Pride is the universal sin." He explained, "Selfishness is one of the more common faces of pride. 'How everything affects me' is the center of all that matters—self-conceit, self-pity, worldly self-fulfillment, self-gratification, and self-seeking." Unless we strive to control these feelings, they will drive us from the path. We know that humility is the antidote for pride. ("Beware of Pride," *Ensign*, May 1989, pp. 4–6.)

Jesus taught his disciples, "If any man will come after me, let him deny himself, and take up his cross, and follow me." (Matthew 16:24.) We take up the cross when we deny ourselves the things of the world and keep the commandments.

As we face our trials and our tests, which are a necessary part of this life, there is great comfort in knowing that he understands. The scriptures tell us: "And he shall go forth, suffering pains and afflictions and temptations of every kind; and this that the word might be fulfilled which saith he will take upon him the pains and the sicknesses of his people. And he will take upon him death, that he may loose the bands of death which bind his people; and he will take upon him their infirmities, that his bowels may be filled with mercy, according to the flesh, that he may know according to the flesh how to succor his people according to their infirmities." (Alma 7:11–12.)

From his example we learn how to carry our cross. Before every important action, at every stage of his work, we find him praying. He prayed with simplicity, with earnestness, and with unwavering trust. He always speaks of God as Father. Our Heavenly Father has told us to pray anytime. Have you ever thought how available he is to us? No appointments, no waiting periods, no scheduling, no callbacks. He is always available. Is it possible that any of us would think to carry our cross without prayer? Might not our load be lightened if our prayers were more frequent and more specific to our needs? Sometimes we say our prayers, but we don't really pray.

In my bathroom, on the wall just below a magnifying mirror that I use to do my makeup, is a small piece of needlework that reads "Woman, where goest thou?" I look at those words at the beginning of each day. When I return at night and stand at the same mirror to remove the makeup, I wonder if I shouldn't have another wall hanging that asks "And where have you been today?"

Maybe on our knees we should ask, "Father, this is thy servant. Guide me in thy steps this day." And at the close of the day we should report on our efforts, give thanks, and seek forgiveness and help when we have fallen short.

I have been to the Holy Land. I have walked where Jesus walked and felt his presence there. But I have also felt his presence on the little Micronesian island of Truk, where a handful of Saints came to the airport because the plane was touching down for just twenty minutes and we couldn't stay. There would not be another plane for several days. These good Saints stood in their humble attire, with little evidence of any worldly goods, holding hymnbooks, and sang from the heart, "Because I have been given much, I too must give." (*Hymns,* no. 219.) They placed flowers around our necks, on our heads, and in our arms.

Recently in our Relief Society class, a sister in a wheelchair was asked to tell what the Book of Mormon meant to her. A sister sitting next to her arose, pushed the wheelchair up to the front of the class, and turned her around. The sister in the wheelchair bore witness of her conversion, her spiritual manifestation, her witness of the Book of Mormon. She wept and we all wept. She didn't have a hanky, so I passed mine to her. She promised to wash it and return it. I pled with her to keep it as a small token of her great gift to all of us. I felt God's presence there.

One very special day years ago, I tucked my little niece Shelly into bed, and clutched in the bend of her elbow was Sweetie-Pie. Sweetie-Pie had all the hair worn off the back of her head, one eye missing, and one arm almost detached, yet there she was tucked protectively under the arm of a little three-year-old. Standing in the twilight with the last rays of the sun filtering through the shades, I looked long and thoughtfully at the quiet child now at rest from her play. Almost reverently I rearranged the covers and bent down to feel both her warmth and that of Sweetie-Pie. When does the preparation really begin? When do mighty souls become great mothers? What of the space between here and there? What of those attributes, skills, characteristics, and spiritual promptings that all become a part of the greatness? When do all the qualities of motherhood, the myriad of bits and pieces and combination of beauty, come together? I observed that little girl hug her dolly, and I felt His presence there.

I remember another significant time. One day when all the world seemed wide open to my younger sister and she was ready to step up and take what it served, she announced to our parents, "I want to help the world turn, and I want to help it turn sharply. I want to make a mark in life." With enough successes already to give her considerable confidence, she could have lofty goals. She was bright and capable—some would say brilliant—and very able. As she spoke of faraway places and exotic endeavors, Dad posed a simple question with a not-so-simple answer: "Shirley," he said, "why don't you become great like your grandmother?"

Like a bird interrupted in flight, she asked with some surprise, "What did she do?"

In a reflective tone with thoughts of one gone for some years now, he replied, "She kept a beautiful home and raised a fine family."

The counsel was brief, yet it seemed to weigh heavily. Being the older sister, I remember feeling that my dad was inspired. My sister now has eleven children, a remarkable family walking in His steps.

I felt God's presence in a letter received not too long ago from a young man who is an inmate in the state prison. He wrote:

> I couldn't understand what interest God would have in someone like me, for I was a drug addict and convicted felon who hadn't prayed or gone to church in almost ten years. Still the feeling persisted, and even intensified, until one afternoon I finally was drawn to my knees in prayer in the privacy of my steel and concrete prison cell. For perhaps the first time ever I opened my heart to God. I said, "Heavenly Father, I know that you are there, but I don't know why. Why would you want to help someone such as me?" And the answer came softly, but so clearly and deeply felt that I've never been able to think about it without feeling it once again and having tears come to my eyes. "Mark, it is because I love you." How inexpressibly wonderful it felt to know that the God of the universe knew me and loved me. I stayed on my knees praying and crying for hours, and from that day on, I was truly a changed person. Not only was my heart changed, but my entire life was changed. With God's help, old habits can be overcome.

Yes, his presence can be felt in the most remote islands of the world, inside prison walls, in neighborhoods, in little girl's bedrooms, and in Relief Society classes.

We feel God's presence when we pray for each other and with each other. Oh, what a spiritual feast we would have if we could gather together and each share an experience when we felt his presence. It might be in the grocery store, in the parking lot, in the dormitory, in the laundry room washing the dirty clothes. Have we learned to recognize that feeling? Did we feel his presence yesterday, today, even now? Most often, it is when we are in the service of someone else that we feel we are in his steps.

I believe St. Francis of Assisi expressed the desire of all of our hearts:

> *Lord, make me an instrument of Your peace.*
> *Where there is hatred let me sow love;*
> *Where there is injury, pardon;*
> *Where there is doubt, faith;*
> *Where there is despair, hope.*
> *Where there is darkness, light, and*
> *Where there is sadness, joy.*
>
> *O divine Master,*
> *Grant that I may not so much*
> *Seek to be consoled as to console;*
> *To be understood as to understand;*
> *To be loved as to love;*
> *For it is in giving that we receive;*
> *It is in pardoning that we are pardoned, and*
> *In dying that we are born to eternal life.*

When we are following in the steps of Christ, it is more than just correct behavior. It is not only what we do—it is what we are. Our attitudes, our motives, our desires, our reasons for doing some things and not others must be driven by a desire to come unto Christ. The world is darkening in iniquity, and if we are to stay on the path, we need reminders of his divine examples.

I carry in my wallet a message that reads:

> When I am hot and rebellious, bitter and cynical and sarcastic; when it seems as though evil can win in the world and the battle is to the strong; when it seems as though pride possesses all the high places, and greatness belongs to those

who can grab the most; when it seems as if faith is mocked, love fails miserably and humility is trodden in the dust; when pity seems weakness and sympathy folly; when a foul egotism rises up within me and would bid me assert myself, plan for myself, serve my own interests, play for my own hand and "take care of number one"; then, O my Lord, may I hear in imagination the gentle splashing of water falling into a basin, and see the Son of God washing His disciples' feet! (Leslie D. Weatherhead, *The Eternal Voice,* New York: Abingdon Press, 1940, pp. 81–82.)

As we move forward on our individual paths with our common goals through our valleys and our mountains, we can expect to be refined through the furnace of affliction. (1 Nephi 20:10.) Let us remember the promise of the Lord: "I will go before your face. I will be on your right hand and on your left, and my Spirit shall be in your hearts, and mine angels round about you, to bear you up." (D&C 84:88.) A well-known story, titled "Footprints," seems to convey the message we're talking about:

One night I had a dream. I dreamed I was walking along the beach with the Lord, and across the sky flashed scenes from my life. For each scene I noticed two sets of footprints in the sand. One belonged to me and the other to the Lord.

When the last scene of my life flashed before me, I looked back at the footprints in the sand. I noticed that many times along the path of my life, there was only one set of footprints. I also noticed that it happened at the very lowest and saddest times in my life. This really bothered me, and I questioned the Lord about it.

"Lord, you said that once I decided to follow you, you would walk with me all the way, but I have noticed that during the most troublesome times in my life, there is only one set of footprints. I don't understand why in times when I needed you most, you should leave me."

The Lord replied, "My precious, precious child. I love you and I would never, never leave you during your times of trial and suffering. When you saw only one set of footprints, it was then that I carried you."

We are away from home, and on occasion we have feelings of homesickness. The way may seem long, but however steep the path, the Lord will be with us. Jesus Christ, our Lord and Savior, set the pattern and invites us to follow him. May we walk in his steps each day of the journey as we seek to do the will of our Father who hath sent us. And on the occasions of our homecoming may we be prepared to report, "I have finished the work which thou gavest me to do."

CHAPTER 19

The Blessings of the Temple

D uring a visit to the historic Kirtland Temple, which was
dedicated in 1836, I stood at the door before entering and
tried to comprehend, even in part, the eternal significance
of all that transpired there in the early history of the Church.
My great-great-grandfather John P. Greene was among those
who helped build that temple. It was built through staggering
and immeasurable sacrifice. It was difficult for people to obtain
the basic necessities for survival, and sickness was not uncom-
mon. Heber C. Kimball told of Sidney Rigdon's intense petitions:
"He frequently used to go upon the walls of the building both
by night and day and frequently wetting the walls with his tears,
crying aloud to the Almighty to send means whereby we might
accomplish the building." (Karl Anderson Ricks, *Joseph Smith's
Kirtland,* Deseret Book, 1989, p. 165.)

The man who supervised the construction of the Kirtland
Temple was Artemus Millet, a wealthy builder from Canada.
History records that the Prophet Joseph Smith said to Brigham
Young, "Brother Brigham, I give you a mission to go to Canada
and baptise Brother Artemus Millet and bring him back here [to
Kirtland]. Tell him to bring a thousand dollars with him." (Ibid.,
p. 16.)

In full faith and obedience Brigham Young went to Canada
and converted Artemus Millet and his family, and they returned
to Kirtland with him, bringing the thousand dollars. This new
convert played a vital role in building "a house of God" where

heavenly messengers visited. God the Father and the Son, Jesus Christ, appeared in the temple. The ancient prophets Moses, Elias, and Elijah came and restored the divine keys of authority so the kingdom of God could once again be established upon the earth.

In the temple Joseph Smith and Oliver Cowdery witnessed a sacred vision. The Prophet wrote:

> The veil was taken from our minds, and the eyes of our understanding were opened.
>
> We saw the Lord standing upon the breastwork of the pulpit, before us; and under his feet was a paved work of pure gold, in color like amber. His eyes were as a flame of fire; the hair of his head was white like the pure snow; his countenance shone above the brightness of the sun; and his voice was as the sound of the rushing of great waters, even the voice of Jehovah, saying: . . . For behold, I have accepted this house, and my name shall be here; and I will manifest myself to my people in mercy in this house. Yea, I will appear unto my servants, and speak unto them with mine own voice, if my people will keep my commandments, and do not pollute this holy house.
>
> Yea the hearts of thousands and tens of thousands shall greatly rejoice in consequence of the blessings which shall be poured out, and the endowment with which my servants have been endowed in this house. And the fame of this house shall spread to foreign lands; and this is the beginning of the blessing which shall be poured out upon the heads of my people. (D&C 110:1–10.)

So intense was the feeling for days and even weeks following the dedication of the temple that many present thought that the Millennium had begun and that all tribulation and temptation were past. The Prophet had to warn them more than once that all they were experiencing was of God, but that the struggle with the adversary and with darkness would be renewed — and that they would know again all the trials that are at the core of saintliness. (*Teachings of the Prophet Joseph Smith*, pp. 160–61.)

While the Saints were building the Kirtland Temple, the Lord was preparing others who would move this great work forward from one generation to the next until the truth of the gospel would, as the Prophet said, "go forth boldly . . . till it has penetrated every continent, visited every clime, swept every country, and sounded in every ear, till the purposes of God shall be accomplished, and the Great Jehovah shall say the work is done." (*History of the Church* 4:540.)

With the dedication of the first temple in this dispensation, sacred ordinances, long withheld, were once again available. From that small and humble beginning, led by a prophet of God, Latter-day Saints have exhibited power and strength and ability to endure trying and testing according to each one's faith in the Lord Jesus Christ.

What is it that impels people to sacrifice all, if necessary, to receive the blessings available only in the temple? It is their faith and a spiritual witness of the importance of our covenants with God and our immense possibilities. In the temple, the house of the Lord, we participate in ordinances and covenants that span the distance between heaven and earth and prepare us to return to God's presence and enjoy the blessings of eternal families and eternal life.

I grew up in the shadows of the Alberta Temple. I remember the stories of my grandfather, Daniel Kent Greene, a man of great faith. A family history records that "on November 5, 1913, the ground-breaking ceremony was held" for the construction of the Alberta Temple, and "Daniel K. Greene, who phoned regularly to see if his help was needed yet, plowed the first furrow for the excavation work and continued plowing for a month."

In the beautiful baptismal font in that temple, I was baptized at eight years of age and then confirmed a member of the Church, and later I performed many baptisms for the dead. It was in the temple at age fifteen that I received my patriarchal blessing, which has provided a guide and a comfort for my life. I remember well when I was sixteen years old being rushed to Calgary for a serious operation in which I was expected, according to the specialists, to lose my equilibrium and my hearing if I lived. My parents, who were faithful temple workers for many years, explained to me with great faith that they were putting my name on the prayer roll in the temple and all would be well. I remember living in anticipation of going to the temple one day and coming to understand how that worked.

We learned to depend on the Lord for good health and a rich harvest, and we also learned to lean on the Lord when there was serious illness and no harvest. Stories of faith were repeated over and over and nourished our growing faith like gentle rain nourished the crops, while severe winters helped teach us of endurance and commitment. From good people one generation ahead of me, I learned about perseverance, fortitude, and stability.

When I was a teenager, the missionaries of the Western Canadian Mission gathered at the temple for a conference, and it was then that I met Elder Heber Kapp. Eventually my fervent prayers were answered, for a few years later we were sealed in that temple for time and all eternity.

Whenever I enter the beautiful Alberta Temple after these many years, thoughts come flooding to my mind. I feel like a child once again at home in the family circle. I almost anticipate the presence of my parents and grandparents. Being there is a wonderful foretaste of the joy we will have when we return to our ultimate home.

President Brigham Young in his writings gives us a glimpse of the blessings for those who make and keep sacred covenants and receive the ordinances of the temple in preparation for our ultimate return home. He wrote: "[God] is the Father of our spirits; and if we could know, understand, and do His will, every soul would be prepared to return back into His presence. And when they get there, they would see that they had formerly lived there for ages, that they had previously been acquainted with every nook and corner, with the palaces, walks, and gardens; and they would embrace their Father, and He would embrace them and say, 'My son, my daughter, I have you again;' and the child would say, 'O my Father, my Father, I am here again.' " (*Journal of Discourses* 4:268.)

In many parts of the world, in many languages, I have heard young women repeating with great feeling the last part of the Young Women Theme, which states: "We will be prepared to make and keep sacred covenants, receive the ordinances of the temple, and enjoy the blessings of exaltation."

Some time ago a young woman came to my office with her mother and grandmother. While the young woman carefully unwrapped a small porcelain replica of the temple, the mother and grandmother stood close by smiling their approval. The young woman explained to me that she had made this small temple and keeps it in a prominent place on her dresser where she can see it every day. Then with a tone of happy confidence she explained, "I always knew that every boy was to go on a mission, which meant going to the temple, and that included my brothers, but now I know that every girl should also prepare to make and keep sacred covenants and receive the ordinances of the temple, so that ultimately we can enjoy the blessings of exaltation."

She had set a goal and provided a constant reminder.

In the temple we receive a review of the entire plan of salvation and realize the blessing of the sealing power that unites families forever. We learn something of our pre-earth life and the purpose of our temporary separation from our Father and his Son, Jesus Christ. During our physical separation from them, we begin to more fully realize the blessings of continuous communication through prayer and personal revelation.

In the temple we can feel the spirit of the Lord. His love and compassion for us become more of a reality when we realize that one day we can return home to our Father's presence and bring our loved ones with us. It is then that the sealing power in the temple and the related blessings become the whole purpose and focus for our life.

In the temple the reality of eternity presses upon our minds. When we learn to view our experiences in this life with the perspective of eternity, we tend to draw away from the things of the world that pull us apart, and to feel closer to the things of the Spirit that keep us whole. We begin to view life differently. We "look not at the things which are seen, but at the things which are not seen: for the things which are seen are temporal; but the things which are not seen are eternal." (2 Corinthians 4:18.)

In the temple we learn to differentiate between the things we must hold to tenaciously and that which we must be willing to let go of if our faith is to grow. We realize that we don't need all of the answers and we don't need additional promises. All we need to get back home, really home, is there for us. The ordinances of the temple are available only in the temple. And are they important? According to Elder Boyd K. Packer, these ordinances "are more than advisable or desirable, or even than necessary. More even than essential or vital. They are *crucial* to each of us." (*The Holy Temple,* Salt Lake City: Bookcraft, 1980, p. 146.)

In the temple we may find peace concerning matters for which our mind has no answers. From the blessings of the temple, we learn that we may be healed spiritually as well as physically.

It is in the temple, more than in any other place, that we learn more about who we are and whose we are. God is our Father. We are his children. And he has provided a way for us to return to his presence. It is in the holy temple that we gain a better understanding of why we are here and what to expect and, more importantly, how to prepare for the return to our heavenly home.

CHAPTER 20

Together by My Hearth

The student body officers at Brigham Young University once sponsored what came to be known as the Last Lecture Series. Students gathered in the garden court in the Wilkinson Center to meet their friends and hear a message from one of their peers. The subject was to be based on what the speaker would choose to say if this were his or her last lecture. Thoughtful insight from serious students always made attendance worthwhile. Often the message was valuable because, through it, one came to better know, understand, and appreciate the messenger.

I have often pondered in my mind what thoughts I would choose to share if given the opportunity to present a last lecture in the garden court; but maybe more important, what might I choose to say in the case of a last lecture or message — not to a crowd, but one-on-one to a friend, a loved one, a family member?

We are not usually permitted to know when our last message might be given, but if we knew, I wonder if our conversation or our tone would be different even when we say a brief good-bye in the morning as we go our separate ways during the day. Would we ever in a hurried moment miss the opportunity to say what later we wish we might have said, given another chance? Might a lecture delivered in a loud voice such as "Don't slam the door when you leave!" be replaced with a message of love? Would a word of encouragement that gives confidence be more sustaining for the day ahead than even breakfast?

If you and I and a few close friends were gathered together

by my hearth, what would you want to say if it were your last message? Not necessarily the last one forever, but even for this week or this month or maybe a year or two until we meet again. I've given this idea some thought. Without the benefit of a conversation in which we could listen and learn from each other, I'll go ahead and share my thoughts. Maybe in another setting you will share your thoughts with other friends.

Thoughts of last lectures, I find, often move from small talk of little consequence, just words, to ideas and feelings that breathe life into words. Hearts are knit together in lasting friendship with a sense of tenderness, caring, and an awareness of a feeling of attachment.

In the book *The Little Prince,* we learn from the fox about attachments:

> "Who are you?" asked the little prince, and added, "You are very pretty to look at."
>
> "I am a fox," the fox said.
>
> "Come and play with me," proposed the little prince. "I am so unhappy."
>
> "I cannot play with you," the fox said. "I am not tamed."
>
> "Ah! Please excuse me," said the little prince.
>
> But, after some thought, he added:
>
> "What does that mean—'tame'?" . . .
>
> "It is an act too often neglected," said the fox. "It means to establish ties."
>
> " 'To establish ties'?"
>
> "Just that," said the fox. "To me, you are still nothing more than a little boy who is just like a hundred thousand other little boys. And I have no need of you. And you, on your part, have no need of me. To you, I am nothing more than a fox like a hundred thousand other foxes. But if you tame me, then we shall need each other. To me, you will be unique in all the world. To you, I shall be unique in all the world . . . "
>
> The fox gazed at the little prince, for a long time.
>
> "Please—tame me!" he said.
>
> "I want to, very much," the little prince replied. "But I have not much time. I have friends to discover, and a great many things to understand."

182

"One only understands the things that one tames," said the fox. "Men have no more time to understand anything. They buy things all ready made at the shops. But there is no shop anywhere where one can buy friendship, and so men have no friends any more. If you want a friend, tame me . . . "

"What must I do, to tame you?" asked the little prince.

"You must be very patient," replied the fox. "First you will sit down at a little distance from me—like that—in the grass. I shall look at you out of the corner of my eye, and you will say nothing. Words are the source of misunderstandings. But you will sit a little closer to me, every day . . . "

(Antoine de Saint Exupéry, *The Little Prince*, New York: Harcourt Brace Jovanich, 1971, pp. 78–84.)

Pull up a chair, if you will, and sit close by my hearth. I'd like to share with you my last lecture, at least for now. I wonder why it is that a desire to reminisce often creeps in when we think about important things we wish to share with people we love. We reach back and begin to remember. Reflections somehow help prepare the way for the message.

As a child I learned a poem by Douglas Malloch that has come to have increased meaning over the years and sets the stage for my thoughts:

> *If you can't be a pine on the top of a hill,*
> *Be a shrub in the valley,*
> *But be the best little shrub on the side of rill.*
> *Be a bush if you can't be a tree.*
> *If you can't be a bush, be a bit of the grass.*
> *Some highway some happier make.*
> *If you can't be a muskie,*
> *Then just be a bass;*
> *But be the liveliest bass in the lake.*
> *We can't all be captains,*
> *There has got to be crew.*
> *There is something for all of us here.*
> *There's big jobs to do and there's lesser to do,*
> *But the task you're to do is the near.*
> *If you can't be a highway,*
> *Then just be a trail.*

If you can't be the sun, be a star.
It isn't by size that you win or you fail,
Be the best of whatever you are.

To be the best of whatever you are says nothing about the need or desire to be better than someone else. This thought removes competition. We do not try to elevate ourselves or diminish others. We feel unthreatened as others strive to be the best of what they are.

The burden of pride is unloaded when we turn to our Father in heaven in humility, knowing that he knows us and knows what we have the capacity to become if we keep our thoughts and feelings centered on our Savior and our individual growth and progress.

This idea of becoming our best self extends far beyond the vision of our own possibilities. C. S. Lewis wrote:

> Imagine yourself as a living house. God comes in to rebuild that house. At first, perhaps, you can understand what He is doing. He is getting the drains right and stopping the leaks in the roof and so on: you knew that those jobs needed doing and so you are not surprised. But presently he starts knocking the house about in a way that hurts abominably and does not seem to make sense. What on earth is He up to? The explanation is that He is building quite a different house from the one you thought of—throwing out a new wing here, putting on an extra floor there, running up towers, making courtyards. You thought you were going to be made into a decent little cottage: but He is building a palace. He intends to come and live in it Himself. (*Mere Christianity,* New York: Macmillan, 1979, p. 174.)

God is our Father. We are literally his spiritual offspring, his children.

The Psalms of David remind us of the majesty of all of God's creations: "When I consider thy heavens, the work of thy fingers, the moon and the stars, which thou hast ordained; what is man, that thou art mindful of him? and the son of man, that thou visitest him? For thou hast made him a little lower than the angels, and hast crowned him with glory and honour. Thou madest him to have dominion over the works of thy hands; thou hast put all things under his feet." (Psalms 8:3–6.)

With an understanding of our possibilities, we strive to be the best of whatever we are and "seek . . . earnestly the best gifts, always remembering for what they are given." (D&C 46:8.)

The tendency to have pride, to compare ourselves with someone else, and to want to be better than another is such nonsense, such a waste of time, such a lack of understanding and faith. Our Father has given us an explanation that, when we fully understand it, helps us appreciate the individuality of each of his children. He explains: "All have not every gift given unto them; for there are many gifts, and to every man is given a gift by the Spirit of God. To some is given one, and to some is given another, that all may be profited thereby." (D&C 46:11–12.)

Peace of mind and contentment come through our daily efforts to follow our Savior and his example. An ancient story from the Far East tells of a young lad in search of truth. After finally making his way to the gates of paradise, he firmly knocks. A voice from within is heard to say, "Who is there?" The lad answers, "It is I." There is no further communication and the gates remain closed. The boy returns to the village disappointed but determined to continue his quest. During his long search, he learns to live in harmony with himself. He puts down hatred, envy, prejudice, fear, and jealousy. He learns to love, to serve, to give thanks, and to praise. Years later, now an old man and having learned the lessons of life, he approaches again the entrance to paradise. A voice is heard to say, "Who is there?" The old man, after a lifelong pilgrimage, responds, "It is Thee," and the gates open wide.

The Prophet Joseph Smith taught, "The nearer man approaches perfection, the clearer are his views, and the greater his enjoyments, till he has overcome the evils of his life and lost every desire for sin; and like the ancients, arrives at that point of faith where he is wrapped in the power and glory of his Maker and is caught up to dwell with Him." (*Teachings of the Prophet Joseph Smith*, p. 51.)

From the lessons of life we learn that our best self unfolds gradually as we learn to attune ourselves to the Spirit and follow the gentle whisperings of the still, small voice.

When I come to my evening prayer and review the events of the day, I am reminded of my weaknesses, and I might become discouraged if I did not understand that perfection is a gradual process and not an event. And yet the Lord instructs, "I would that ye should be perfect even as I, or your Father who is in heaven is perfect." (3 Nephi 12:48.)

Is it possible, one might ask, to ever hope to attain such perfection? And if so, through what process? Surely if this question could be answered, it would guide me to be the best I can be and guide you to be the best you can be. There is an answer. We know it as the process of sanctification, by which we become clean and pure and holy. Through the grace of our Lord and Savior, Jesus Christ, following baptism we can begin this holy process step by step as we expend our own best efforts.

It is comforting for me to remember the teachings of the Prophet Joseph Smith concerning our striving for perfection in this life. He said: "When you climb up a ladder, you must begin at the bottom, and ascend step by step, until you arrive at the top; and so it is with the principles of the Gospel—you must begin with the first, and go on until you learn all the principles of exaltation. But it will be a great while after you have passed through the veil before you will have learned them. It is not all to be comprehended in this world; it will be a great work to learn our salvation and exaltation even beyond the grave." (*Teachings of the Prophet Joseph Smith*, p. 348.)

As we seriously contemplate being the best that we can be, so far as our own limited perspective allows us to ever imagine, I believe that the vision of our possibilities opens up to glorious vistas as we come to understand where we are along the path, where we want to be, and how to get there.

Consider, if you will, a sheet of paper divided into thirds.

Let the first column on the left represent where we are, the challenges of today, the reality of our mortality. The column on the far right represents where we want to be, to be sanctified, to be worthy of immortality and eternal life. The space between where we are and where we want to be represents the process, the steps we must take to become our best selves, clean and pure in a state of holiness, sanctified.

First let us consider where we are. A prevalent attitude of our day is suggested by someone who said, "We want to live in Zion but to maintain a summer home in Babylon." This attitude is reflective of one whose spirit is willing but whose flesh is weak. When the vision of eternity presses upon our minds and we are guided by the Spirit, we learn to view life differently. The demands of the flesh become submissive to the Spirit as we become our best selves.

Under the heading "Where We Are," I have written on my sheet a scriptural reference, Ether 12:27. We learn that our Father in heaven gives us weakness so that we may be humble. "My grace is sufficient for all men that humble themselves before me," he says, "for if they humble themselves before me, and have faith in me, then will I make weak things become strong." In that same column, I have added Jacob 4:7 to remind me that the Lord God shows us our weakness so that we may know that it is by his grace that we can accomplish all things. Surely this knowledge expands the vision of our possibilities, increases our hope, fortifies our faith, and strengthens our determination.

In the third column, under the heading "Where We Want to Be," I have written the reference 3 Nephi 27:20–21. We begin to comprehend at least in part our immense possibilities after we repent and are baptized: "Ye may be sanctified by the reception of the Holy Ghost, that ye may stand spotless before [our Father in heaven] at the last day." Repentance allows Christ's atonement to be an active part of our lives and help in the process of sanctification.

Closing the gap between where we are and where we want to be is seldom done in large steps; rather it is done in small increments, little by little, day by day. After consistent effort over a period of time, we can look back and marvel at the growth that has been made. We don't remember the day we learned to walk, nor do we remember the time when the mighty change of heart took place and we have no more desire to do evil but to do good continually, a state of saintliness that is attained only by conforming to the laws and ordinances of the gospel.

When I have a better understanding of where I am and where I want to be, my concern and attention rest with the process, the daily steps that move me steadily forward. In the center of the page, which represents the process, I have written Helaman 3:35: "Nevertheless they did fast and pray oft, and did wax stronger and stronger in their humility, and firmer and firmer in the faith of Christ, unto the filling their souls with joy and consolation, yea, even to the purifying and the sanctification of their hearts, which sanctification cometh because of their yielding their hearts unto God."

Is this understanding for our own good, to save our own soul? Yes, but also to become true disciples in every sense of the word and more effective in every possible way in helping to bring souls unto Christ; these result as we become the best of whatever we are and assist others to become the best of whatever they are.

In consideration of a last lecture containing a message of greatest worth, it is easy to identify with Alma: "O that I were an angel, and could have the wish of mine heart, that I might go forth and speak with the trump of God, with a voice to shake the earth, and cry repentance unto every people! Yea, I would declare unto every soul, as with the voice of thunder, repentance and the plan of redemption, that they should repent and come unto our God, that there might not be more sorrow upon all the face of the earth." (Alma 29:1–2.)

Consider the setting and circumstance of the "last lecture" given by Moroni. He had given his life in the service of mankind according to the will of the Lord. He was left alone in sorrow and sadness for the wickedness of his people, yet in his heart he carried a desire to use his last breath in leaving a message that would one day be instrumental in bringing thousands, even millions, of people unto Christ:

"I had supposed not to have written more, but I have not as yet perished; and I make not myself known to the Lamanites lest they should destroy me. . . . Wherefore, I write a few more things, contrary to that which I had supposed; for I had supposed not to have written any more; but I write a few more things, that perhaps they may be of worth unto my brethren, the Lamanites, in some future day, according to the will of the Lord." (Moroni 1:1, 4.)

"Yea, come unto Christ, and be perfected in him, and deny yourselves of all ungodliness; and if ye shall deny yourselves of all ungodliness, and love God with all your might, mind and strength, then is his grace sufficient for you, that by his grace ye may be perfect in Christ; and if by the grace of God ye are perfect in Christ, ye can in nowise deny the power of God.

"And again, if ye by the grace of God are perfect in Christ, and deny not his power, then are ye sanctified in Christ by the grace of God, through the shedding of the blood of Christ, which is in the covenant of the Father unto the remission of your sins, that ye become holy, without spot." (Moroni 10:32–33.)

In my mind I have imagined sitting together with you by my hearth taking turns reading the scriptures, sharing insights, bearing testimony, and developing lasting ties, while rejoicing in the knowledge that through the process of sanctification, our Lord and Savior makes it possible for our ties of friendship to be eternal in nature. When parting company for a few hours, a few days, or longer, may our thoughts always express love and hope and faith, always looking forward in anticipation of being together again, remembering, "That same sociality which exists among us here will exist among us there, only it will be coupled with eternal glory, which glory we do not now enjoy." (D&C 130:2.)

Our joy will be found in our eternal relationship, knowing that God is our Father and that as his children we can become joint-heirs with Jesus Christ, our Savior and Redeemer.

Index

Adversity. *See* Trials, tribulations, testing
Advertising and immorality, 157
Agency, free, 61, 137
Airport, experiences at, 91, 92, 99
Alberta, Canada, 33, 122–23, 136
Alcoholism, 24, 157
Alma, 32, 38, 81
"As Sisters in Zion," 94
Atonement, 77, 85, 87–88, 187
Attitude, 37, 97

Ballard, Melvin J., 76
Baptism, 104, 137, 177, 186
Behavior, changing, 35
Benson, Ezra Taft, 93, 135, 139, 168
Blessings: to those who serve, 28–29; patriarchal, 142, 166, 177; for obedience to commandments, 149; of eternity, 177; of the temple, 178, 180
Blind man, story of, 34–35, 36
Brigham Young University: student who was unprepared at, 49; lighting the "Y" at, 57; traditions of, 58; service at, 60–61; Last Lecture Series at, 181
Buck, Bertha, 86

Cannon, Elaine, 25
Cannon, George Q., 53, 166, 167
Charity, 32, 35, 40, 98

Charlie Brown, 131–32
Charlotte's Web, 103–4
Chess game, and choices, 8
Choices: burden of, 4; in relation to values, 5; in chess game, 8; and material possessions, 9; between essential and nonessential, 12; and hope, 36; and influence, 52; to do the Lord's will, 53; right, and gratitude for Jesus Christ, 77, 79–80; letter from prison inmate about, 150–51; determine personal values, 158; can conquer a "cricket," 159
Coal stove, and priorities, 33–34
Commandments: and love, 19; as source of light, blessings, 72, 159; repentance and commitment to keep, 135; baptismal covenant to keep the, 137; obedience to, 140, 146, 149, 168
Commitment, 9–11, 109, 135, 156
Communication: with God, 85; and rural telephone system, 122–23; lack of, story of young woman and mother, 123–25; importance of, with God, 126–29
Conscience, 80–81, 150, 151
Consequences, 5–6
Conversion, 14–15, 170
Courage, 155, 158
Covenants: understanding of and

191